BUSINESS TIME MANAGEMENT STRATEGY

JOHN LOK

ISBN 979-888591998-2

Contents

Preface

Introduction

I write this book aims to let readers to feel why and how that if one organization can manage its time how to arrange employees to work, then it can bring positive consumer emotion and build good consumer behavior to prefer to choose to buy its product or consume its service. In my this book, I shall indicate some cases to explain how and why effective organizational time management ought may raise customer sale or service number. The topics include as below:

Chapter 1: I shall explain how organizational effective transport time management can reduce warehouse goods delivery time and increase customer satisfaction , in this chapter has four cases to explain how effective transport time management can let customers to feel satisfacion. These cases include: First case, warehouse transport time management case, in especial when goods are needed to deliver to overseas when goods can be transport to overseas from one week to three days or less day by air plane. Second and third cases, also I shall explain how public transport tools, e.g. bus drivers and taxi drivers effective driving time management, when they can drive their buses to arrive bus stations on time or taxi station in order to avoid passengers to feel angry and they prefer to choose other kinds of public transport tools to replace it to catch, e.g. mass underground train, ferry , train, tram etc. other kinds of public transport tools. The fourth case, I shall explain how effective salsespeople sale time managment ,e.g. how to introduce products to customers , it can raise whose sale number. It concerns how sale time management games model solves salespeople emotion problem in store environment.

Chapter 2 : Reducing front line staff time pressure. I shall explain why and how organization can reduce front line staffs to feel workload when they need to contact many customers, e.g. in airline front service check passport traveller serive staffs, in airport restrict security check passport airport service security staffs, entertainment theme park entertainment facility queue crowd control service staffs etc. Also, I shall explain how and why stores can reduce time pressure to let front service staffs to work, then they may build good customer relationship. When organizations can let any front line staffs to feel less time pressure when they need to serve many customers and they need to reduce long time to queue. Then, customers‘ emotion will be better.

Chapter 3: Effective hospital time management strategy, i shall discuss how one hospital's effective time management can avoid any hospital visitors won't find any car park vacancy in hospital car park when they have need to park their cars in the hospital car park or reduce workload pressure to front line hospital service staffs, e.g. nurses, register counter service staffs. when they need to serve many patients or patient's families or friends in the long queue time.

Chapter 4 : Time management concerns how teachers and students manage themselve between learning and teaching time and private time in order to raise student learning effort. I shall indicate what the time management factor can influence the final grades of academic students. I shall give examples to explain why time management can influence the final grades to be bad of academic students easily. Time managment can link between sleep time quantity and learning time arrangement, the relationship between physical fitness time and learning time arrangement.

Chapter 5: I shall explain that a national chain of restaurant how to apply mobile advertising time management method to persuade or attract restaurant eaters, e.g. travellers to choose its restaurant to eat when they arrive the country. Why can the short time restaurant mobile advertise attract overseas travellers to choose the restaurant to eat in preference? Does the short time restarant mobile advertise influence the travellers' restaurant choice in preference when they run on their mobiles to see the restaurant's advertise concerns its location and meal choice and price from their short mobile restaurant advertise message?

Prologue

Table of content

Reference

CHAPTER ONE

Organizational effective transport and sale time management

Case 1
How time management reduces transport cost of shipping or road transportation to the most minimum level in warehouse, factory locations linear programming management science solution method :
Researching the main shipping or /and road transport problem to bring cost rising to between either warehouse or/and factory or both and the goods transfer transport destinations.
Inventory Models management science method helps warehouse, factory locations to reduce road or shipping transporation cost between goods transfer locations. For certain types of inventory control problems, certain models that attempt to minimize the cost associated with ordering and carrying inventories have been developed.
Transportation problem is a particular class of linear programming, which is associated with day-to-day activities in our real life and mainly deals with logistics. It helps in solving problems on distribution and transportation of resources from one place to another. The goods are transported from a set of sources (e.g., factory) to a set of destinations (e.g., warehouse) to meet the specific requirements. In other words, transportation problems deal with the transportation of a single product manufactured at different plants (supply origins) to a number of different warehouses (demand destinations). The objective is to satisfy the demand at destinations from the supply constraints at the minimum transportation cost possible. To achieve this objective, we must know the quantity of available supplies and

the quantities demanded. In addition, we must also know the location, to find the cost of transporting one unit of commodity from the place of origin to the destination. The model is useful for making strategic decisions involved in selecting optimum transportation routes so as to allocate the production of various plants to several warehouses or distribution centers. Suppose there are more than one centers, called 'origins' , from where the goods need to be transported to more than one places called 'destinations' and the costs of transporting or shipping from each of the origin to each of the destination being different and known. The problem is to transport the goods from various origins to different destinations in such a manner that the cost of shipping or transportation is minimum. Thus, the transportation problem is to transport various amounts of a single homogenous commodity, which are initially stored at various origins, to different destinations in such a way that the transportation cost is minimum.

Inventory Models Management Science Solution Method

A tyre manufacturing concern has many factories located in many different cities transport cost case

For certain types of inventory control problems, certain models that attempt to minimize the cost associated with ordering and carrying inventories have been developed. The objective of the transportation model is to determine the amount to be shipped from each source to each destination so as to maintain the supply and demand requirements at the lowest transportation cost.

For example: A tyre manufacturing concern has many factories located in many different cities. The total supply potential of manufactured product is absorbed by retail dealers in different cities of a country. Then, transportation problem is to determine the transportation schedule that minimizes the total cost of transporting tyres from various factory locations to various retail dealers.

The transportation model can also be used in making location decisions. The model helps in locating a new facility, a manufacturing plant or an office when two or more number of locations is under consideration. The total transportation cost, distribution cost or shipping cost and production costs are to be minimized by applying the model. How do you calculate the cheapest way to ship goods between several warehouses and stores? In this lesson, you will explore the transportation problem and its solutions.

Searching What Is The Transportation Problem to cholocate retail stores case

Mathematical Programming Management Science Solution Method: It attempts to maximize the attainment level of one goal subject to a set of requirements and limitations. It has extensive use in business, economics, engineering, the military and public service, mainly as an aid to the solution of allocation problems.

Imagine yourself owning a small network of chocolate retail stores. To run a successful business, you will also have to own or rent a warehouse where you will store the goods ready to be delivered whenever the stores need them. If you have only one warehouse, it will be supplying all your stores. However, as soon as you expand and open a second warehouse, you will have to make an important decision: which warehouse will deliver which goods to each of your stores? Depending on the choice you make, you might save or spend a significant amount of money.

The transportation problem is a distribution-type problem, the main goal of which is to decide how to transfer goods from various sending locations (also known as origins) to various receiving locations (also known as destinations) with minimal costs or maximum profit. As long as the number of origins and destinations is low, this is a relatively easy decision. But as the numbers grow, this becomes a complicated linear programming problem. Think about Walmart. In 2016, it had 5,229 stores and 166 distribution centers in the US! It would be impossible to calculate the optimal shipping routes without a computer algorithm.

General transportion problem types

Transportation problems can be classified into different groups based on their main objective and origin supply versus destination demand. Transportation problems whose main objective is to minimize the cost of shipping goods are called minimizing. An alternative objective is to maximize the profit of shipping goods, in which case the problems are called maximizing.

In a case where the supply of goods available for shipping at the origins is equal to the demand for goods at the destinations, the transportation problem is called balanced. In a case where the quantities are different, the problem is unbalanced.

When a transportation problem is unbalanced, a dummy variable is used to even out demand and supply. A dummy variable is simply a fictional warehouse or store. For example, if total supply at all warehouses is 50 units, but total demand at all stores is only 40 units, we create a fictional store with an additional demand of 10 units. The cost of shipping to the fictional store is usually zero. Now, the transportation problem becomes balanced. It is worth noting that sometimes problems that are solved using the transportation method have nothing to do with an actual movement of goods. What is crucial for applying the method is to recognize the network of connected elements.

Case 2

Time management science solves public transport passenger queue problem

Waiting Line (Queuing) Models: solution imbalanced taxi and passenger queue in urban public transportation service case

The Four Problems Of Urban Transportation (And The Four Solutions)

The fixed-route bus and the bicycle solve at least one urban problem better than new technologies urban transportation problem case. There are four main problems in urban transportation that require four separate solutions. Some urban transportation design recommendion argued that technology can solve some problems, but not the same problem that public transit solves."The city has four separate problems of urban transportation which have four separate kinds of solutions, and it is very important to not mistake the solution for one problem for the solution for a different problem."

The first solution :

Bus stop time real -time information technology and apps solution method

Friction arises between a transit system and its users when the users don't have the information they need when they need it. That problem has been largely solved, Walker said, by information technology and apps. "That has been a fantastic transformation. Some of you may not be old enough to remember what life was like without real-time information, when you just went right out into the snow and wondered when the bus was coming."

The second solution:

Innovation method

The innovation method solves the city has four separate problems of urban transportation may include: Emissions and Energy Efficiency: "for which we're currently working on electric vehicles, and that's fantastic." Labor and Safety: The cost of labor is the primary driver of operation costs for passenger transport, Walker said. "It is why your bus doesn't come more often, and it is also why Uber can't make money." Autonomous vehicles will address that and the accident rate. "There is a problem with the efficient use of labor, and also a colossal problem of safety for which we are talking about autonomous vehicles, and that's fantastic." Space: "And there is a fourth problem which is the efficient use of space, for which the solution is on the one hand, cycling and walking, and on the other, public transit provided by big vehicles."

The third soution:

The fixed-route bus or train solutione method is the best solution reason

The fixed-route bus or train is the vehicle of the future, because it remains the most efficient way to move large numbers of people through the congested space of a city. In his critique of public transit, Musk pointed out that people prefer "individualized transport, that goes where you want, when you want," like the Tesla Model S. But Walker contends individualized transport that goes where you want when you want can't move people through a congested city as efficiently as a fixed-route bus.

"We are always going to need vehicles sized to the appropriate capacity requirement, which means big buses in big cities," he said. "Our friends in the tech industry, including many of you here, and I love what you're doing, are always trying to sell us stories about how everything will fit together into a magnificent fusion. They want us to mix it up, to think about how it combines. And I'm always saying, but wait a minute, if you're going to be a smart customer you have to think about how they work separately as well."

Instead of above technological methods to solve public transport problem. The queue control management method will be one good solution How do I conduct queue management of passengers in waiting taxi or bus area for Public transportation Vehicles?

Are there existing design projects and studies that a public transportation vehicle (Taxi or Bus) would know the number of passenger in waiting area/ shed through long range network? I am conducting a design project for buses in my country that would know the number of passenger in waiting area and this information will be sent to the terminal or bus which will they used to pick up these passengers. Thus, congestion of buses and passenger can be lessen

I think that there are 2 technical issues: a) how to collect and transmit information, b) how to manage public transportation to minimize queue. About the 1st question you probably need either to do it manually (operator sitting at every station and making phone calls like "please send one more bus urgently, we have 100 of people waiting here", but this may be too expensive, at least for city buses) or to do it automatically (video camera, some image recognizing software that calculates people and then sends a message to the center) in this city has four separate problems of urban transportation concerns taxi and bus queue case.

Conclusion of the best solution method

As I know, there is not such a system design yet. but you may devise one by using the queue theory and optimizing the performance of the system by the following pattern:

- defining a objective function corresponding to the total passengers awaiting time.
- optimizing the objective function by finding the best set of assigning the available buses to the stations (considering the routes)

Case 3

Time managment waiting Line (Queuing) Models: solution imbalanced taxi and passenger queue in airport case

Predicting Imbalanced Taxi and Passenger Queue Contexts in Airport management problem

For certain types of problems involving queues, special descriptive models have been developed to predict the performance of service systems such as car garages – cars standing in queue for servicing.

The taxi and passenger queue contexts indicate the various states of queues related to taxis and passengers (i.e. taxis are waiting for passengers, passengers are waiting for taxis, both are waiting for each other, none is waiting). Predicting these queue contexts in a future time is very important for better airport ground transport operations. However, queue context prediction at the airport is a challenging problem due to the presence of different contextual factors i.e., time, weather, taxi trips, flight arrivals and many more. Also these taxi and passenger queue contexts at the airport are imbalanced since some of the contexts are very infrequently occurring compared to others. In this paper, we address the problem of predicting imbalanced taxi and passenger queue contexts at the airport. First, we investigate different contextual factors, including time, taxi trips, passengers and weather for queue context prediction. Then we propose a detailed step by step solution to address this problem. To support the effectiveness of our detailed approach, we generate a queue context dataset by fusing three real world datasets including taxi trip, passenger wait time and weather condition that represent the taxi and passenger queue contexts at any major international airport in any country City. The experimental results demonstrate that our developed queue context prediction

framework provides detailed solutions to deliver higher accuracy in queue context prediction.
Therefore, context-aware mobility analytics enables the provision of intelligent analysis on mobility contexts considering different user perspectives. The success of many applications such as transport management and location recom- mendation requires the discovery of valuable knowledge through extensive analysis of related factors . For example, an airport can be regarded as the first and last impression of a city. Since a longer passenger wait time for a taxi ride can diminish the satisfaction rating of an airport , the authorities try hard to maintain a higher customer satisfaction rating by providing various mobility services such as easy and comfortable airport transfer to the city using taxicabs. However, the demand-supply equilibrium of taxis is highly dependent on the taxi drivers‘ decisions to make airport trips. The ubiquitous data can help with managing the mobility of airport users by detecting different mobility contexts (i.e. situa- tions of the concurrent queues related to passengers and taxis) . The intelligent analysis and prediction of different mobility contexts can help with making mobility decisions for airport passengers and taxis at different times of the day.
We argue that by incorporating the temporal deviation of taxi drivers' moves as the feature importance score can identify good quality neighborhoods and thus significantly boost the taxi-passenger queue context prediction accuracy. We utilize a real world queue context data set that includes information from taxi trip logs, airport passenger arrivals and weather conditions which are relevant to the different queue contexts. Then we propose a temporal driver-knowledge deviation based feature importance scheme to select a quality neighborhood for predicting taxi and passenger queue contexts.
As we extract more features by computing the deviations of all feature values from its hourly mean along with the current features of the queue context dataset , it is necessary to check the relevancy of all features. The reason is that the use of all these features may degrade the prediction performance significantly due to the inclusion of some irrelevant and redundant features. Also, for different stations, the configurations such as lane numbers, and maximum queue length of taxis and passengers can affect the solution of the passenger-taxi queue problem.
The proliferation of pervasive devices in smart cities has enabled the development of many smart mobility applications . Smart parking is one of the innovations that provides easy to use parking services to the urban

commuters by leveraging pervasive sensors and flexible payment systems. Inferring a situational awareness map using clustering methods has become a popular research topic in recent years. GPS trajectory has been utilised in smart mobility applications. In this section, we briefly review the related work which can be separated into two categories: points clustering and trajectory clustering. For example, intelligent reminders of user activities and notifications for major transporta- tion delays due to the current situation of the users. This outcome can also be leveraged for the applications of discovering user rou- tines based on personal contexts of mobile users. In an intelligent healthcare scenario, a robust and simultaneous recogni- tion of multiple user contexts would be important to be considered for elderly and disabled people, while travelling through various accessible paths .

Case 4

Sale time management games model solves salespeople emotion problem in store environment

Any organizations can let salespeople feel happy to sell their products. Then their sale performance will also raise. The question concerns that how to make them to feel happy to help the organization to sell their products? I shall explain how to apply managment games or management psychological methods to solve this organizational problem as below:

How to manage sales for predictable revenue?

In order to hold salespeople sale psychology whether they feel happy or unhappy, executives need to understand the essential activities, sales managers must focus on to be analysts for change, foster continuous improvement and create a sales culture that drives results. Sale executives need to know how to achieve top objectives of sales management is to drive sales, capture new revenue and exceed monthly sales and margin objectives, e.g. performing sale strAregy development with each salesperson on Monday morning at a minimum, and in a formal one-on-one meeting during the week;using strategy tools and questioning techniques to ensure the prospects are qualified and the strategy is valid; knowing the ratio between future values and future monthly quotos to raise sale opportunities; six month on-going sale plan aims to make sure there are coordinated to achieve sale to various market segments; developing on ongoing series of networking events to build market awareness in order to ensure all salespeople attend specific events involved in networking by salespeople to, understanding the market how to influence salespeople sale method to sale number, understanding trends and seeking some channels to raise additional sales opportunities; how to create trained or warm sale environment to let sales teams feel happy to sell.

How to design and utilize efficient control sale procedures?

The sale cycle procedure may include these market activities, such as advertising, sales promotion, market research, physical distribution, pricing , sale place, sale staffs seeking. SO, any organizations need have good sale planning, direction and control of the personnel, selling activities of a business with including recruiting, selecting, training, rating, supervising, paying or reward system, motivating strategy , as all these tasks apply to the personnel sales-force.

The factors may influence salespeople psychology, they may include fair income reward system, or appreciation methods and sale career development plan to every salesperson. It aims to encourage them to achieve the highest sale effort. Anymore, methods to train sale managers have the right direction to guide, lead and motivate their salespeople, e.g. knowledge of salespeople psychology needs how to satisfy them, understanding why they choose to do or act themselves sale behaviors in order to improve their weakness to motivate salespeople to achieve company's sale target goal every month easily, e.g. raising profitability, sales volume, market share, growth and corporate image building raise clients' confidence to choose to buy this company's any products more easily.

The sales organization is required for the following purposes, they may include: enabling top-management, to devote to more time in policy making for the growth and expansion of business to divide and fix authority among the subordinates , so that they may shirk work, to avoid repetition of duties and functions, so that there may not be any confusion among them to locate responsibility of each and every employee , so that they can complete the whole work in stipulated time, if not then the particular person must be responsible, to establish the sales effort to enforce proper supervision of sales force.

What does the concept of salespeople replacement value mean?

What is a sales force turnover management tool?

Sales force turnover is defined as the rate at which salespeople leave an organizations, resignations, retirements or dismissals. So, if the organization can raise the sales force turnover ratio, because many salespeople can be promoted or the retirement, or the sales force turnover ratio raising reasons as well as they are not resignation or dismissal reasons. I believe that the organization ought have good sale environment and reasonable reward and welfare strategy to let its salespeople feel happy to help this company to sell its products every day.

However, sales management's actions have direct or indirect effects to impact on turnover. Direct effects may include the firm's firing or dismiss policy. The indirect effects on sale turnover may include new salesperon recruiting and selecting policies affect the quality and performance of the sale force as well as the speed at which salespeople are replaced. The same policies have an impact on the sales force turnover rate through the characteristics of the newly recurited salespersons and the promotion , training, retraining policies, support, supervision, compensation. ALl of those factors have an impact on salesperson's personal satisfaction or dissatisfaction absolutely. So, any sale organizations need to concern how and why whether any one of above these factors may influence their salespeople how to perform or act sale behaviors in order to excite their sale number more effective in long term.

How to achieve sale force management effectively?

Sale management is one strategy to many organizations, because organizations expect their salespeople can only raise product sale number. So , they will consider whetther how to implement the sale management strategy to be the most suitable to themselves sale organizations in order to excite their sale teams to sell their products to achieve sale growth aim effectively. So for organization's long term sale growth development, it seems that one excellent sale management strategy can help the organization has stable sale number growth in long term possible.

However, the term " selling" includes a variety of sales situations and activities. For example, those sales positions where the sales representative is required primarily to deliver the product to the customer on a regular or periodic basis. The emphasis is this type of sales activity is very different to the sales position where the sales representative is dealing with sales of capital equipment to industrial purchasers. IN additions some sales representatives deal only in export markets whereas others sell direct to customers in their homes. So, sale organizations need to sell to local or overseas market as well as its target customer is businessmen or individual consumer or both in order to implement to choose their most suitable sale management strategy to train their salespeople more effective or achieving sale growth objective only. Because these its sale major target and where sale market place both factors will influence how it ought train its salespeople, so any organization's training method ought be influenced to change by whom is its major sale target and where is its major sale market location factors.

How to know the psychology of salesmanship?

When the organization can predict or find reasons to explain why its salespeople feel unhappy to help
this organization to sell its products. Then, it can attempt to improve its weaknesses in order to let its salespeople to feel more sale service satisfactory feeling to continue to help this organization to sell its products. Then, it won't need not often to train or recruit new salespeople to replace its old salespeople in consequence.

How to know what its salespeoples' real need in order to raise their sale service satisfactory feeling ?

Psychology means that " science of the mind" and psychology plays to important part in business and it is quite worth to bring to influence any organization salespeoples' posivitive or negative sale emotion in their every sale process between themselves and their every client in personal. For example, if the salesperson often have negative emotion or he feels unhappy in every sale process, then he will encounter or increase many times of sale failure possibilities. He will feel that he is one poor verbal advertiser or seller or promotor to help his organization to promote its products to sell again as well as he will lose confidence to sell any products next sale chance, because his failure sale experiences are accumulated to influence his sale emotion to be poor or difficult sale.

Hence, the poor performance salesperson needs have more successful sale experiences to compensate his / her prior many sale failure times feeling, if the organization hopes this poor performance salesperson can raise sale number easily. Overall, any organizations need to concern how to improve or raise the more failure times of sale experience salespeoples' sale techniques or methods or attitudes more than choose to fire or dismiss them as well as finding another new salesperson to replace him/her. Because it is possible that the salesperson 's poor sale performance that is not due to himself/herself poor sale effort and sale knowledge or lacking sale experience to the product, it may be due to the poor sale team cooperation relationship , feeling poor or not comfortable sale physcial shop environment, poor sale manager and other salespeople working relationship, the sale manager lacks leadership effort, poor family relationship etc. external factors more than himself/herself personal poor or negative emotion or poor health etc. personal factors. Hence, the organization ought enquire him/her why he/she feels unhappy to sell its products and it needs to attempt to find methods to solve his/her challenges immediately. If his/her challenges can be solved. It is possible that his/her sale efforts can be also raised for. So, if the organization can know how to utilize positive sale emotion psychological methods to predict or know why and how every salesperson perform his/her sale behavior in whose daily sale tasks, then it can concentrate on implementing effective and the most suitable sale training to raise their sale abilities more easily.

However, the sale training may include: How to build or improve long term good salesperson and his/her customer sale service relationship between every salesperson and every client in every buying and selling cycle process, how to using right communicating styleds for better understanding every client's real needs, powers and negotiating, e.g. every salesperson needs to review why there are many clients do not choose to buy any products from his sale presentation or promotion, finding every time sale failure reasons can let the salesperson makes himself/herself sale failure reasons evaluation or judgement in order to find what is the major reason influences his/her sale failure, e.g. lacking product knowledge, he/she often let many clients to feel that he lacks patience to listen the client's enquiry or feedback, his sale presentation is not attractive to let many clients like to stay longer time to listen his sale presentation in whole sale process, the salesperson himself/herself emotion is negative and he /she can let many clients feel he / she is not happy or does not enjoy to sell this product from himself/herself face impression or sale behavior impression easily, lacking enough sale techniques to persuade his/her clients why he/she ought choose to buy this product in whole sale process etc. these factors may influence the salesperson's sale failure chance to be raised. Hence sales manager ought need to spend long time to meet the poor sale performance salesperson to discuess what his/her sale challenges are the most major to influence his/her every sale successful chance in order to improve his/ her sale performance more successfully.

In conclusion, the reasons why salespeople often encounter sale failure possibilities. The factors may include these aspects, such as they lask the desire to help customers to make satisfactory purchase decisons, they only concern how to achieve sale final objective or aim only, it will cause clients feel they do not real concern their real needs. They only concern to sell the product in success. They do not know how to describe the product whether what characteristics or features it owns accurately in order to increase sale chance to persudade them to make final decision to by the product, they do not attempt to participate the whole sale process to help them to choose the most right product in order to satisfy their any purcahse needs, they ought avoid deceptive or manipulative influence tactics, avoid the use of high pressure sales techniques etc. Thus, if any organizations can spend time to investigate what factors cause why any one of salespeople choose perform his/her sale behavior often in order to know or understand their salespeople' sale psychology absolutely. Then, I believe that their sale number will only grown more easily.

Image

CHAPTER TWO

Reducing front line staff time pressure

● Time Pressure Influences Shopper Behavior

To research consumer behavior, it has different theory to explain why and how the consumer is influenced to make the choice by different factors. For example, utility theory,it explains that consumers make choices based on the expected outcomes of their decisions. They are viewed as rational decision makers and they only consider self interest.

Utility theory views consumer is as a " rational economic man". However, the factors influence consumer behaviors may include these activities, such as need recognition, information search, evaluation of alternatives, the building of purchase intention , the act of purchasing choice, consumption and finally disposal. Hence, it seems that all the consumer's activities in whose purchase processes. They will influence their choice. For example, when the property purchase consumer , he plans to research different kinds of properties information concern price, location, housing areas, room numbers, building facilities and environment facilities. He will find some sample target properties information to make comparison in order to decide to buy which of property is the most suitable to satisfy his living need.

However, it is not only one activity for the property purchase buyer in his decision making process. It also include evaluation of alternatives activitiy when he ensures the accurate property information number in order to evaluate whether which one of all these property choices is the most suitable one. Hence, it explains that property information research and evaluation of alternatives both activities are needed to spend much time for this property buyer. If he does not plan to find one property to live in short time, it is possible that he can spedn one month, even more than one month or more than three months time to do the only property information gathering activity.

Hence, it seems that time factor is not the main factor to influence the property buyer to do property purchase decision immediately. Otherwise, if the property buyer plans to find one new property to live within one month. Then, time factor is possible one important factor to influence this property purchase chocie decision. For example, if he felt that he needs more time to spend to gather information concerns the large house area size and the properties have more than three bathrooms and/or bedrooms properties information. Then, he will be possible not to find any this kinds of all property information. So, it means that all these properties won't be his choice. It is because long time property information gathering activity factor influnce.

I assume that the property buyer is a economic man and he does not spend much time to do the property information gathering activity. So, this kind of property needs him to spend long time to gather properties inforation in order to make this kind of properties comparison. Moreover, because he expects to live one new property within one month. So, he only chooses the properties, they have less than three bedrooms and/or bathrooms to gather sample properties information in order to make property purchase decision within one month. Hence, the time variable factor can only influence the property purchaser when he/she needs to make decision to buy one new property to live in the short time. If some kinds of properties choices number has a lot and the property buyer feels to let that he/she must need to spend long time to find the suitable properties number to make evaluation alternatives comparison behavior.

Then, the time variable limiting pressure factor will be possible the main factor to influence the property buyer's choice in order to make the most suitable kind of property purchase decision. Hence, it is one case example of how time limiting pressure factor can influence consumer purchase choice decision, such as property purchases market case. The reason explains why the property buyer needs to spend time to do property information gathering. I assume that general property buyer behave rationally in the economic sense. They won't only believe property agent individual property photos advertisement , it concerns where the property location is and facility etc. information on property photos in order to evaluate whether the property price is reasonable to pay. Generally, property buyers need to attempt to gather property information and visit the different actual property locations to make choice. So, general property consumers would

have to be aware of all the available different kinds of properties consumptin options from themselves properties information gathering and the properties agents' verbal properties introduction both be capable of correctly rating each property alternative and the available to select the optimum course of the final property purchase action.
Hence, in the property purchase and sold market, limiting time pressure factor will be important influential factor to decide whether the kinds of properties will be option to some property buyers when they feel need to find one suitable property to buy in short time. Otherwise, in some food consumption market , time limiting pressure factor will not be the main factor to influence consumer option. Such utility theory indicates consumers are as one rational economic man, whom do not expect to spend much time to do any options evaluation decision making.
However, in coffee market, buying a coffee comes almost automatically and does not need much information search. Hence, time limiting pressure factor won't one main factor to influence coff consumer to choose to buy the kind of coffee to drink. However, there are other factors to influence coffee consumers' kind of coffee drinking option from cultural, social, personal or psychological factors. So, coffee taste producer can follow these factors to estimate how coffee consumers might behave in the future when making any kinds of coffee making purchasing decisions.
Firstly, social factor can affect coff consumer behavior significantly. Every coffee consumer has someone around influencing his/her coffee buying decisions. The important social factors include reference groups, family, role and status , e.g. when the coffe buyer has high income job and his friends have good educational level and high income. Then, he will compare his reference group, such as his friends' coffee buying behavior choosing which kinds of coffee taste to drink in habits or lifestyles. If he chooses the kind of coffee taste to drink, its price is cheaper to compare his friends' drinking coffee tastes. Then, he may be influenced to follow his friends to drink the same kinds of coffee taste in order to keep their same social status and role between him and his friends.
Secondly, the coffee consumers will be influenced how to choose which kinds tastes of coffee to drink by personal factors, such as his age, life cycle state, occupation, economic situation , lifestyle and personality and self-concept. Age related factors are such as taste in food, e.g. the kinds of coffee taste. Although, coffee price is cheap, but if the coffee consumer's income is more and he/she can often spend to buy different kinds of taste coffees

to drink. Then, his/her income level will have much purchasing power to influence his/her purchasing behavior. Hence the coffee consumer's frequency of consumption of different kinds of coffee taste drinking choice behavior will represent whether his/her income level is high or low in possible. For example, the consumer needs to go to automatic coffee shop to buy at least three cups or more different kinds of high class good taste coffee brands to drink per week. Although, these high class coffee brands‘ prices are higher than the low class of coffee brands. But the coffee consumer still only buys any one of these kinds of high class brands' coffee taste to drink. Hence, it seems that this coffee consumers ought have high income to let hims to buy at least three cups of high class brand of coffee taste to drink from automativ coffee ship per week.
So, income factor can influence the coffee consumer to choose either coffer purchase from supermarket or coffee drinking at automatic coffee shop. If the coffee consumer only chooses to buy coffee from supermarket, due to the bottles of different kinds of brand coffee can provide more different tastes of coffees choices from shelves to let him to buy to drink at home. So, it seems that the coffee consumer's income level is low in general. Otherwise, if the coffee consumer only chooses to go to automtic coffee shop to buy the high class brands of coffee tastes to drink at least thre times or more per week. It may mean that the coffee consumer has high income level to support him/her to often go to automatic coffee shop to buy different kinds of high class coffee tastes to drink frequently every week. Som high or low income level factor can influence every coffee consumer individual drinking coffee behavioral options.
Moreover, when the coffee consumer is younger coffee consumer will be possible to buy much coffee to drink. Because younger age people can accept to drink coffee habitually more than older age people. Also, it is possible that younger peopler feel often drinking coffee behavior will help them to bring more health feeling and /or raising nervous to learn , due to they need often to go to schools to study. Otherwise, older age people feel often drinking coffee behaviors won't help them to bring more health and they do not need to raise nervous to learn.
Finally, even, cultural difference factor will influence coffee consumers number fo any countries. For example, western countries'people like to drink any kinds of coffee tastes traditionally. Asia countries' people like to drink any different kinds of teas tastes traditionally. So, different kinds of teas tastes will be asia people's traditional drinking substitute to replace

different kinds of coffee tastes more easily. Hence, culture difference will be one factor to influence asia coffee buyers number. So, it seems that time limiting pressure factor won't influence coffee consumers' coffee taste choices to different kinds of high class or low class brands, visiting coff shops or visiting supermarkets choices, frequent or not frequent coffee drinking behaviors.

● How and why time limiting pressure
influences consumer choice

Can consumer buying decisions be influenced by time limiting pressure. For these three situations, they will influence consumer hoe makes different buying decision, e.g. in the little time available, but the consumer needs to do more effort needed to choose to buy which kind of product among variety kinds of product choice or in a moderate amount of time available, or a considerable amount of time available. In this first situation, the consumer can not real attempt to find any weaknesses or unique characteristics of the products, because it has no enough time to allow whom to choose. So, his/her product evaluation won't be th most accurate to satisfy his/her needs because little time can only allow him/her to find some weaknesses of the products. Otherwise, in the final situation, because the consumer has a considerable amout of time to allow him/her to attempt to find the weaknesses and/or strengths characteristics of the products choice. So, he/she ought do the more reasonable or accurate evaluation of these products to choose the most effective economic beneficial product to buy. Thus, it seems that time limiting pressure factor can influence the consumer to make more rational or more reasonable economic beneficial consumption decision making to buy the product or consume the service.

Thus, a consumer buying decision will require these situations to do buying decisions, they may include either little time and conscious effort or a moderate amount of time and effort or a considerable amount time and effort. The products may include cheap products/services , e.g. fruit, DVD, university courses, computers, facial services, surgeries, sport shoes, reference books, soft drinks, magazines as well as expensive products/ services, e.g. cars, houses, luxury goods, e.g. jewellery, female hand bags, holiday travelling entertainment. So, any expensive or cheap products or services, the consumer will need to spend either little or moderate or considerable amount time to do gathering information about the different kinds of products or services in order to find which brand of product or service can bring more economic benefit when he/she chooses to use the product or consume the service. He/she will compare his/her preference sample brands limiting number of products or services choices to decide to buy the brand of product or consume the brand service easily. However in the consumer's consuming decision making process, he/she will need to spend either little or moderate or a considerable amount of time to do the evaluation and choice consumption behavior. It means that time limiting pressure factor will influence the consumer how to make consumption choice consequently.

What are the impacts of reduced branding on consumer choice and time limiting pressure to influence consumer behavior? When one consumer needs to choose products to buy one in a time limiting pressure consumption environment, when branding on packaging is reduced, e.g. the brand of product has 10 different style of packages to let consumer choice, but it reduces to only 5 different style of packages to let consumer choice. How does it influence the consumer decision making when the consumer has little time to allow to choose these 5 different style of packages ? For example, when the consumer expects to spend only 10 minutes to choose any one style of package to buy drom this brand product. Currently, this brand of produxt has reduced different style of packages number from 10 to 5. Do you feel that the consumer will feel easy to do decision making to choose to buy the most attractive style of package product from this brand's 5 different style of packages choices? Is 10 minutes consumption choice time enough to let the consumer to make final purchase decision from these brand's 5 different style of packages choice? Will the time limiting pressure be reduced , due to this brand's 10 style packages are reduced to 5 style packages to let the consumer to choose within the 10 minutes expected limiting consumption choice time.

It is one interesting psychological consumption behavior to research whether the brand's reducing different style of packages number factor will influence the consumer to do the decision making in the short time in the time limiting pressure environment. For toothpaste, shapmo products example, if the brand of these products' style packages choice is reduced to 5 style packages from 10 style packages choice. When one consumer finds the brand of toothpaste or shampo has only 5 style packages on the shelves in supermarket. If the consumer has moderate or considerate amount time to let him/her to choose these both kinds product any one style of packages to buy. The 5 style packages to these both inds of products will be impossible to satisfy the consumer's choice need because he/she haas much time to stay in supermarket to choose. Otherwise, if the consumer has little time to allow to stay in the supermarket , e.g. ony 10 minutes. Then, he/she expects to spend only 10 minutes consumption choice time to do buying decision making within 10 minutes. These both kinds of the brand's products, its styl of packages choice number is reduced to 5, it is possible to satisfy the consumer's choice need to buy this brand of product either toothpaste or shampoo and both of thee brand of products to be chose to buy in the supermarket. So , the reducing style of package number to let consumer choice will be seem to let the conumer to do buying decision making in the limiting time pressure consumption environment.

In fact , package is such a visual to influence consumer decision making in the short time or personal limiting time choice process. If the product has more attractive package design, the it can bring more attention effort to influence the consumer to choose to buy the product in the short time information transfers to influence the consumer decision making to choose to buy more easily , when he/she is active in communication process. So, package, communicating with consumer in the selling place , has become an essential factor to influence the choice of consumer.

Scientific researches have proved that package decisions can attract consumer attention, transfer the desirable information abou tthe product, position , the product in consumer conscious, differentiate and identify of among similar kinds of products. In that way elements of package influence consumer decision making process and can determine the choice of consumer and the package itself can become more competitive advantage.

However it is not absolute that the brand of product has more package choices, it must have more customers to choose to buy its product. For example, there are two brands of shampoo in the supermarket shelf. One brand shampoo has 5 different style of packages and 5 different fruit productive elements to cause similar fresh fruit smells to attract consumers to buy. Another brand shampoo has 3 different style of packages and 3 different fresh fruit smells to attract consumers to buy in the same shelf location also. When one supermarket customer has little time to expect to stay in the supermarket, e.g. he expects only to stay the supermarket maximum to 15 minutes. he expects to buy one bottle shampoo and meats and fruits and vegatables within 15 minutes. Hence, he expects only to spend about 5 minutes to choose one brand of shampoo product as well as he demands to spend maximum 10 minutes to buy other foods within 15 minutes. When he stays in the shampr shelf location, he finds only two

brands of shampoo products are displayed on the same shelf location. One brand of shampo has 5 different style packages to let him to choose, but he feels that these 5 diffeent style packages are not very attractive. Otherwise, the another brand of shampo has only 3 different style packages to let him to choose, but he feels that the 3 different style packages are very attractive. Due to he feels time causes pressure to choose these two brands of shampoo immediately. So, he does not want to spend more time more than 5 minutes to choose on brand of shampoo to buy. He will be influenced by the brand of different styles of packages more attraction to influence his buying decision making obviously. So, whether the shampoo brand's package is attractive or not, it will influence the consumer's buying decision making to choose either to buy the brand's shampo product in preference.
So, the more packages choice to the brand's product which may not mean that it has high opportunity to influence consumers' attention. Otherwise, the attractive package element if more important to compare right number of packages choices. Consumer package can influence these elements, e.g. colour, size, imageries, graphics, materials, smell, brand name, producer/ country, information, special offers. Of the brand of products can have much attractive elements. Then, it can attract consumers to choose to buy the brand's attractive package products in short time decision making process, such as perception of needs, search for information , evaluation of alternatives, decision making, behavior after purchase. Such as supermarket case, I assume that any supermarket consumers do not expect to spend much time to choose which brand of product is the most suitable or earning more economic benefit to buy when they need to stay the shelf to need spend much time to select which brand of product to buy in the supermarket. Because in general, supermarket consumers ought plan to buy more than one kind of product or food, even more usually. So, limiting time pressure factor will influence their decision making. Similarly, as my explanation indicates why although, the product had attractive package elements and its has many packages number choices, but it does not mean that it can win the similar product which has not more attractive packages, even it has more packages choices number to let supermarket consumers to choose. So, an attractive package element factor will have more influential and potential to cause supermarket consumers to choose to buy it in the supermarket limiting time pressure consumption environment.

● How the time consumption pressure
factor influences irrational consumption

decision making
When one consumer has a large number of options, he/she will feel time pressure to cause whose accurate and reasonable evaluation. Then, the personal time limiting pressure factor will bring these questions: How does the time limiting pressure influence the consumer evaluation? Will the consumer personal limiting time pressure bring advantages and / or disadvantages in whom consumption decision making? How to help the consumer to solve short time decision problem when he/she encounters extreme time pressure an dchoice overload?
I shall assume every consumer is general one economic man. He/she feels time is important, he /she does not want to spend much time to choose one brand of product to buy among a number of brands of products choices. I also assume that any consumers decision making satisfaction, which is based on search until they found a sufficiently good item, or run not of time. So, it seems that which the consumer needs to buy one kind of product, but the product has a lot number of different brands to let the consumer to choose. The consumer ought need to spend much time to make choice decision making. However, consumer is one economic man, he/she ought not to search all different brands to decide whether which brand of product can bring the much economic value or utility value to choose to buy. So, in general, consumers will only choose sample brands of products to decide to buy the satisfied brand of product. For example, when the consumer needs to buy one television. The television has 20 brands of similar televisions to let he to choose. He will not spend much time to search these similar 20 televisions information. He will only gather sample 10 to 15 or less different brands of televisions to compare what their strengths and weaknesses, unique characteristics. Then, he will make decision to choose to buy the best television from these sample televisions. Hence, in general, consumers will feel time pressure when they feel need to spend much time to choose a lot different brands of similar products. Because they feel time is not enough to let they can do other important matters when they need to spend much time to do search information behavior when they need to buy any products ususally. Hence, it is general consumers psychology that they will feel real choice under time pressure and choice overload, when they have too much a lot of similar brands of products to let them have opportunity to choose to make decision making to buy only one brand of product.
However, when a brand of product is familiar and given its simplicity and familiarity to general consumers' acknowledgement. It will have perference

advantage to attract or influence consumers‘ attention or consideration. So, when the market has similar different brands of products are available to let consumers to choose. The largest choice set is not large enough to create overload to influence the brand's sale when consumers need to spend much time to choose these different brands similar products to buy. Because when the brand's any products are familiar and given its simplicity and familiarity to general consumers' knowledgement. Then, it can build utility confidence to influence general consumers , it will be preference sample brand of product to do buying making option. Hence, the brand's familiarity factor will influence general consumers‘ preference buying decision making option. So, any product manufacturers need to concern how to build its brand familiarity to let many consumers to acknowledge in order to raise its competitive effort. Raising brand's familiarity may be a good method to solve consumer individual choice under time pressure overload , because when the brand of product is preference sample brand to any consumers. It's sale opportunity will also be raised. So, it brings the question: How can the brand of products can cause general consumers' preference choice. For food example, food brands were more likely to choose the implicitly preferred brand over the explicitly preferred one when choices were made under time pressure.

Imagining one customer enters a supermarket 10 minutes before closing time. He failed to write up a shopping list. So, when the staff is preparing to close store at the night, the consumer hurry trys not to for set too many of the ingredients for dinner . What brands of products , he opts for, as he can choose from a variety of similar foods, but time is short and the staff is looking at the consumer impatienty? It is possible that the consumer will probably quickly decide in favor of the foods he likes best, pay, and leave the evening.

Hence, supermarket consumer's first time feeling to the brand of food will influence whom choice. One target category and one attribute category share same response key: Pleasant vs unpleasant feeing, if the supermarket consumer has pleasant feeling when he sees the food photos and touchs the package of the brand of food to feel pleasant in the short supermarket closing time. Then, his pleasant feeling will be chooses to buy the brand of food to eat. Thus, the consumer individual pleasant or unpleasant feeling factor will influence whom consumption choice, such as this supermarket closing time pressure consumption.

In fact, many factors may influence whether consumer behavior is under more or less control. Hunger may influence control in the domain of eating behavior . So, such as the supermarket will close soon,it has store closing time pressure to influence the consumer needs hurry to make choice decision to buy food. If the consumer feels more hungry, he will not spend much time to find the right food to buy. He will be influenced by the different brand's food packages whether which brand of food package can bring a more pleasant to let him to feel, when he touchs and sees the brand of food package. He won't spend time to search whether the different kinds of brands of foods have how much different health elements because the supermarket will close store soon. So, he only depends his individual pleasant feeling to make final food purchase decision. If he feels all of the kinds of brands foods are unpleasant food packages when he sees and touchs them first time as well as he does not feel much hungry. Then, it is possible that he won't choose to any one food to eat. He will choose to go to restaurant to get dinner to replace buying food to cook to eat dinner at home at the night.

The another case is that time pressure concerns how on choice of information source impacts purchase decisions. When the consumer who buys one product , he needs to use the same number of information sources to search the product's information regardless of time pressure. Because he has more available time, he devotes more time , but only to selected the right sources to search information about the product. He will mostly use marketing dominant sources, e.g. magazine. he feels magazine can give more accurate information concerns to the product's good or bad quality real more reasonable and fair evaluation to let the consumer to acknowledge. so, when the consumer has much time to choose to buy which brand of product is the most best choice. He will buy magazine to find information. He believes magazine has more fair evaluation to different brands of product. It won't mislead consumers to make wrong decision making. Hence, in general, when consumers have much time to find information source to search which brand of product is more value to buy. They will attempt to buy consumer magazine to acknowledge whether the different brands of product , which have unique characteristics, strengths or weaknesses in order to compare them to make more accurate evaluation to choose to buy which brand of the kind product. When they have no time pressure to influence their choice process time to be shortened or reduced. Otherwise, these consumers will depend on newspapers, television, radio advertisments information sources when they feel time pressure controls their consumption choice decision making process time to be shortened or reduced. Hence, time pressure will be possible to influence consumer individual information source channel choice.

● Time pressure consumption decision making process characteristics

How we can predict or know the consumer time pressure in whom decision making process? Will it bring advantages or disadvantages to influence the businessmens' benefits? I shall indicate some different consumption situations or environments to explain what will be impacted to sale number is increased or decreased to businesses when the consumer feel time pressure to avoid whom behavioral consumption to the product or the service.

Firstly, I shall explain that what effects of product popularity and time pressure on online shopping behaviors are . Electronic ecommerce is popular to any countries, in special, US, UK, China large areas countries, because when one customer feels need to spend one hour even more time to catch any transportation tool to arrive the shop to buy the kind of product. Then, due to far distance reason, he/she will choose to apply internet to buy the kind of product . If the seller has website to let the consumers to choose online shopping. However, it seems that online shopping behavior can reduce the consumer individual time pressure, when he/she feels need to catch any kinds of transportation tool to arrive the shop to buy the product. Moreover, when the consumer can turn on home computer to enter its website to choose the styles of the kind of products, which one is the most situable to choose. He/she can spend time to search the different styles kinds of product information to compare and evaluate which brand of product will b whose purchase choice easily at home.

Hence, in psychological view, he/she can feel that spending time to search information from internet behavior which is more valuable and it can bring more economic benefit to make final purchase decision more than the behavior of spending long time to catch any transportation tools to visit the shop. Moreover, it is possible to bring failure risk that he/she wastes time to catch any transportation tools to visit the shop if he/she can not find any one of suitable product(s) to choose to buy. Hence, it seems the online shopping can influence the consumer reduced time pressure and wastes time to do any shopping decision.

This is online shopping's attractive strengths to the consumers when they need to spend long time to catch any kinds of transportation tools to visit the shop or when the consumer feels hurry to do other important matters, he/she can not allow himself/herself to spend long time to do his/her visiting the shop behavior. Moreover, another online shopping's advantage is that product popularity can be perceived by examining the information presended on websites. For example, research on onlin reviews confirms the review quantity presented with products become positively influences to consumers' purchase intention and it can persuade the online visitor can make decision to buy the product when he/she has enter the seller's online website to find the most suitable product to choose to buy more easily. Hence, it seems that it is more easy to persuade the online visitor to make final purchase decision more than visiting the shop , when the online visitor can attempt to do the click mouse behavior to enter the seller's online shop, such as website. Then, he/she will be influenced to view the seller's different kinds of colourful and attractive product pictures from the seller's wesite.

Consequently, it has much opportunity to persuade the consumer to do the final purchase decision. if the seller's website is attractive to persuade him/her to visit its website to find any new products more than five times, even tem times or every weak several times , even day one time frequently visiting behavior from internet channel. Hence, due to internet is convenient tool to let consumers to find any product informatons from the seller's website at home or public library , computer, or mobile phone. Consumers must find any product informations any time in any places easily. So, online shopping can reduce any consumers' time pressure to visit any shops to expect to achieve final consumption decision aim in possible.

Thus, it seems that online shopping method can influence consumers to feel time saving and time presure reducing consumption both advantages more than visiting shops' shopping method when the consumer is living far away from the shop. When the consumer feels that he/she is experiencing situational time pressure, then, he/she will respond well to seek another time saving situational consumption environment. So , it explains when one consumer feels he/she has no much time to catch long time transportation tool to visit the shop on the day. When he/she has computer at home, he/she will attempt to type the shop name to research whether it has online shopping platform service from internet. Because he/she does not want to spend one hour, even more time to catch transportation tool to arrive the shop, when he/she can't walk to the shop in short time. Even, he/she may

feel online shopping behavior won't influence his/her eating , sleeping, or recreational time to be reduced at home or any places , when he/she can behave the online shopping behavior at home or any where conveniently.
Consequently, promoting online shopping is as a time-saver is likely to be effective for these experiencing situational time pressure. Those with situational pressure would almost certainly welcome anything that would reduce their activity level and the demands on their time. In fact, there is really no adult learning method for store shopping because it is something everyone learns to do from early childhood. But for many adult consumers, they feel have interest to learn how to use internet and web to shopping. Some adult will feel interest and it is value to learn how to use internet channel to anticipate the complexity of shopping online. For example, Super Walmart cheap frocery store that carries many thousands of products and brands to let online shoppers won't feel confused when viewing its online merchant's home page with only a few menu items and links from its website. So, Super Walmart website can let online shoppers to feel difficult that they can save much time to enter any merchants' home page . They only need to view the Super Walmart's website ,then they can find any preference cheap grocercies to compare and evaluate which one(s) is (are) value to buy. So, Super Walmart's website can let global cheap grocery online shoppers feel it can help them to save time to find any merchant's products from internet conveniently. Consequently, online shopping will be one popular time saving consumption channel to reduce time pressure to some consumers nowadays.
Secondly, I shall explain that what determines purchase decisions for airline tickets when the traveller fees time stress. When a travelling planner has no enough time to prepare whose travelling journey, whether the time stress will influence he/she feels decision difficulties and frustration, when it will cause he/she needs to gather significant amounts of information to lead to make to choose which airline ticket is the most right choice? How and number of airline options and time pressure influence the airline ticket buyer's purchase decision?
However, there are both kinds of time pressures to influence the airline ticket buyer's airline choice decision, they focus on either real decision deadlines (physical time), such as the journey beginning day is any day of this week or tomorrow or subjective feeling of pressure with time (sense of urgency or psychological time), such as the traveller expects that he/she fears all airlines' all seats are full booked in this month. Moreover, he/she

can plan to catch air plane to travel next month. So, he/she will attempt to gather any airlines' tickets prices, flight day and time and destination arrival and weather information in this month to avoid that it is too late to delay his/her next month travelling plan.

Hence, it seems that the effect of number of airlines choices and air tickets purchase deadlines (physical time limit) will influence how the traveller or air ticket buyer's purchase decision using secondary data to search of airline ticket. for example, if the traveller felt time is no enough to let him/her to go to travel agent to enquire any airlines' air tickets prices and seats and date and time air plan departure available time to concern the traveller's destination choice. Then, he/she will be probable to choose to buy electronic-ticket (e-ticket) from internet. If he/she has computer to link internet to gather any airlines' flying date and time and seat available information at home easily. Hence, it seems that one time pressure traveller will be probable to choose e-ticket purchase at home in preference. If the airline can provide online e-ticket purchase option to the time pressure traveller. Due to the pressure time traveller feels closer to departure, the negative impact of number of airline options is not as strong when he/she can view the airline's website to find the flight date, time and seat available information to purchase e-ticket to prebook the date and time to departure the traveller's country and to arrive his/her travelling destination information from the airline's website channel at home or anywhere any time conveniently. Hence, travel agency can bring a positive relationship between airline number of options and pre-booking airline that immediate possibility. When the time pressure traveller hopes the airline can build the good interactive relationship between number of options and decision time limit (number of days till planned travel effort on e-ticket purchase probabilities. So, if the airline website can let the traveller to predict when date and time is accurate available to arrive whom frequently destination choice country as well as the e-ticket's real price , it is not e-ticket preductive price and the real seats number available, it is not the estimated seats number available on the departure time and date to the travelling or arrival country destination. Then, all of these online information to the airline, which will raise the e-ticket pre-booking purchase chance to let the e-ticket buyer to make whose final e-ticket purchase choice decisin to win its e-ticket competitors easily.

Consequently, a real time e-ticket information can attract any time pressure e-ticket buyers to choose to buy its e-ticket (electronic airline ticket) more than visiting travel agent's paper airline ticket option when the travel feels hurry to buy airline ticket to travel in short time.

● Reducing time pressure consumption methods

How can sellers persuade consumers to choose to buy their products or consume their services in time pressure environment easily? It is a valuble research topic to concern how to know how consumer individual decision making to spend his/her available resources (time, money and efforts, or consumption relatd aspects) as well as how any why he/she chooses the preference brand to buy its any kind of products or consume its services, when he/she chooses to buy the brand of products or consume its services? Hence, marketers need to obtain an indepth knowledge of consumer buying behavior.

In any buying process, time factor will have about 10 % to 40 % to influence consumer decision. When the consumer feels hurry to consume, e.g. planning to go to travel, when he/she needs to choose to buy which airline's air ticket and what day and time is the right air ticket prebooking purchase decision right time choice; or enrolling which school to be choosed course to study decison, e.g. how long time is needed to be choose which school is the most suitable to provide the most suitable courses studying choce change; purchase warm clothes to wear in winter, when is the suitable time to choose to buy the cheaper warm clothers to prepare to wear in winter, e.g. Jan to Mar., April to June, July to Aug. month; when is the most suitable time to buy another new house to live, when the property consumer(buyer) has lived present house for long time, e.g. three years or more. All of these issues will include time factor to influence the consumer feels when he/she ought choose to buy the kind of product or consume the kind of service. However, the other factors will also include to influence his/her decision, e.g. family, friend relationship factor, advertising factor, social status factor, cultural difference factor, personal psychological need level or satisfactory level factor, young or old age factor, income level factor, economic environment factor, material enjoyable need factor etc. factors.

However, time pressure factor will be the consumer individual intrinsic (internal) psychological feeling factor, and it is the consumer individual intrinsic feeling to judge whether when he/she ought spend some money to buy the kind ofcnew product or the kind of consume service (what time is the most reasonable or the most suitable time) to make purchase choice decision. However, when the consumer feels hurry to make purchase decision. So, he/she will not hope to spend more time to gather more information to compare and evaluate which one is the right brand of product tochoose to buy or the right service to consume among different brands of products or services. Otherwise, if the consumer has more time or he/she can make the decision to buy any brand of product. Then, he/she ought spend more time to gather more information to compare and evaluate which one is the most suitable product choice to buy or which one is the right service choice to consume. So, time pressure factor will have some influence to any consumers to make decision about what time is the suitable time to buy the kind of product or consume the service. For example, heater product is usually when winter weather time, the heater products need number ought increase in winter weather time or season. But, it is possible that the heater products need number won't increase in winter season / weather possible, when one country , there are many householders or families , they have one heater number at least at home. Then, it is possible that these householders or families won't have consumption desires to buy one more heater product to use in winter at home, because they have had one heater to use at home in winter. So , when the country has have many customers number, they are using the kind of heater products at homes. Most people own at least one heater number factor will have possible to influence enough time available to cause they do not feel hurry to buy any heaters to use at homes, so, their do not feel time pressure to buy any heaters in short time. Because they do not plan to buy the kind of product to use at home in short time when they have one heater product at least to use at homes in present.

Hence, it brings this question: How to attract or persuade the customers, they are using the kind of product to let they feel time pressure to make decision to buy another new or same brand of product to replace to use? The product's better quality , long durable time useful, brand loyalty and past good purchase experience factors will influence him/her to feel time pressure to need to buy another new product in short time. So,when the consumer feel time pressure to make decision to purchase, he/she will choose when is the most right time to gather information, search, select, use and dispose of another new product to replace the old product in the short time.

Hence, the brand of product needs have good product motives, may be raised to the consumer's impluse, desires, considerations which make the buyer purchase the brand's new product to replace the present using product in order to achieve whose satisfactory needs to emotional product motives and rational product motives both. Moreover, persuading or encouraging the consumer feels he/she has real need to buy the kind of new product or replace the present old product (s), the brand of product marketer needs let the consumer feels these any one of nature of motive to raise his/her purchase decision desire in time pressure environment. The natures of motive may include: When the consumer feels desire for saving money, he/she will choose to buy it when the brand of product falls down, when he/she feels fear to be sickness, retirement, he/she will choose to buy insurance policy, when he/she feels pride, or high social status knowledgement, he/she will buy premium product , e.g. gold, expensive watch, car , when he/she feels fashion need, he/she will move house to live from rural to urban, or rural people imitate urban to learn to do their fashion living behavior, when he/she feels possession need, he/she will feel need to buy antiques for its future unique worth satisfactory feeling in possible, when he/she feels health need, he/she will choose to buy health foods, join memebership in health clubs, when he/she needs to enjoy comfortable feeling, he/she will feel need to buy micro-oven, washing machine to use at home, when he/she feels love and affection need, he/she will buy gift items to give to whose friends or families for presents in their birthday or lover day etc. special days to let they to feel happy. So, when the marketer can touch the consumer individual different nature of motives to satisfy his/her personal purchase feeling need and it can know how to influence them to feel that they have these any one of purchase motive needs in short time. Then, they will be persuaded to raise time pressure to make purchase decison to buy any kind of products in short time.

However, instead of attractive good product quality method can attempt consumers to make time pressure consumption behavior. The another method is brand loyalty building method, which can be attempted to encourage or persuade consumers to feel consumption desire need to make decision to buy the brand of any products in time pressure consumption environment. For example, when the consumers feel the brand is loyalty and it can build good image to his/her feeling , and this time pressure factor can inlfuence this brand of any products which has high discount price to attract the consumer individual attention , e.g. familiar brand high class cars, the good confident house agent's high class houses, and the expensive and infrequently buying items, come under this category. When their prices are fallen down to sell cheaper , e.g. twenty per cent discount or more than twenty percent discount sale price than the other similar competitive brands' any products' normal prices. Then, it is possible to let these expensive items' consumers have high involvement and high feeling need in time pressure consumption environment. Because they assume that this discount sale price will be short time sale price, e.g. after three months or next month etc. short time discount sale price in short time period. Then, these expensive items' prices will be raised to the normal sale price, even higher price. so, they have time pressure feeling to feel that it is right time to make consumption decision in order to avoid to lose these low price purchase benefit in this unpredictive cheap discount price purchase items. so, if the expensive item marketer can build long time good brand loyalty relationship to consumers. Then, it will have much influential effort to persuade consumers feel consumption desires need by its any extensive items in the unpredictive short term discount period, due to they do not want to loss this large discount purchase price chance. So, short time discounted sale price, it is another method to persuade consumers to choose to buy the brand's any products in short time pressure consumption environment.

The another persuading time pressure consumption method is that it can let consumers to think more habitual buying the kind of products. products like stationery, groceries, food etc. fall under this category. For example, when the consumer fees the brand of any products ,he/she has habitual purchase experience, of he/she feels that the brand's any products won't sell in market temporary, even he/she can not buy it to use again. Then, it is possible to infuence him/her to feel immediate purchase need to buy a lot of product or food number to keep to use or eat later in the time pressure environment, e.g. the food consumer buys the brand of any breads to eat in supermarkets habitually, but in this moth, he/she watchs TV advertisement to be acknowledge this brand of any breads won't be bought from any supermarkets as soon as possible. Hence, it is possible to influence him/her to plan to make choice to buy a lot of number of this brand of any breads in order to keep the enough of this brand of breads number to eat later. So, this brand of any breads sale loss in supermarkets that will cause the habitual food consumers of this brand of breads, whom make consumption choice to buy a lot number of this brands any breads in short time suddenly. Because they are eating this brand of any kinds of breads habitually. They feel much eating need to lot number of this brand of any breads in short period, because it can satisfy their habitual taste needs of this brand's any kinds of breads. So, brand loyalty and habitual consumption to the kind of product or food , ehich will result simply from the habit and it can influence the consumers feel consumption need to buy the brand's any kinds of products or foods when they feel that they may not buy it again or they can not earn discount advantage after the short time. So, any one of these sale strategies will have possible to raise the consumer individual consumption desire to the brand of products in the short time pressure consumption environment. Also it needs to spend much time to gather information in order to make purchase decision, because the brand had built confidence to consumers when they feel this brand's any products or foods are better to compare the similar brands' any products or foods habitually. So, time pressure consumption environment will persuade them to feel consumption desire to buy this brand's any products or foods in short time. When, they fer that they can not buy any more for this brand's any kinds of products or foods or discounting price in this final short purchase time.

In conclusion, these factors can influence consumer behaviors to be changed to feel time pressure need to do purchase decision making behavior from encough time gathering information available feeling behavior. They have these same views, e.g. habits and routines are very influential, particularly for behaviors repeated daily in a semi-automatic fashion. The consumer's past purchas experience to the brand's products, positive or negative emotion to the brand's products, and the brand's familization, recognition are strong influence , the information available , it is the consumer's mind and the relative important information given to let the consumer knows form different advertisement medias matters for decision making, greating between pieces of information and can be influenced by personal psychological timing limited pressure, the consumer's comparison to differences in price or other characteristics, many pursue value (or in bargain), and compare to alternatives or past knowledge, consumer personal greater value on the immediate future and heavily disocunt future costs or savings to the brand of product, feeling simple and easy decision making process to the product , it can lead the consumer to avoid to spend long time to make purchasing decision and the consumer will easy to choose to buy the product when he/she feels have a loss value if he/she does not decide to buy the product in the short time. SO, it seems that when the marketer can motivate the consumer's consumption desire to feel saving money, promote health, avoid waste time and less nervous workload to gather information for comparison and evaluation alternatives aim. It is seen favorably by the consumer personal time pressure purchase decision making and sense of justice influence factors.

However, sociologists have categorised the motives for consumption behaviors in the short time by the fundamental consumption decision making needs or wants which they satisfy, e.g. having a clear understanding what benefits, characteristics, economic value to the brand's any products , feeling consumption decision making process is a leisure activity. These drivers for consumption behaviorw will either bring positive or negative to influence the consumer personal emotion, either owning enough time available or time pressure environmental impacts can be seen to influence whether the consumer feels he/she needs how long time to be spent to make comparison and evaluate alternatives in order to make final purchase choice in whom decision making process. Hence, the consumer himself/herself time pressure consumption decision making feeling, it can bring positive purchase choice influence,when the marketer can build brand loyalty to let many consumers to feel in the market. Otherwise, if the marketer can not build brand loyalty to let many consumers to feel, but consumers feel time pressure to compare and evaluate its any products to other similar brands of products in the competitive market. Then, its products may be not the preference choices the many customers among the different brands of products choices. So, building long time brand loyalty relationship to satisfy consumers' needs, it will bring positive preference purchase choice to raise the sale effort to the brand of any products when consumers need to make purchase choice in time pressure consumption environment, e.g. seasonal discount sale period, products or foods shortage supply period, without any forever sale possibility in market. Hence , it seems that brand loyalty building factor will influence any brands of products /foods /service sale or provison number to be raised or reduced in possible. Also, it can explain why and how it has close cause and effect relationship between time pressure consumption environment and the brand loyalty building to the brand of products/foods/services to any marketers nowadays.

- What are the in-store and out-store factors influence supermarket fast moving consumer decision

It is one interesting question: How can the brand of product seller influence the supermarket/store fast-moving consumers' more visual attention when the supermarket/store visitor is hurry to make decision to choose to buy which brand of product in time pressure environment? Supermarket/store fast-moving consumers do not usually spend much time to say in any supermarket shelf locations to choose numerous similar alternative brands of products. However, I assume the fast-moving supermarket/store consumer's decision is dependent on the interaction between the supermarket different shelf location sale environment and the mind of the consumer. So, the eye tracking explores this rapid processing that lacks conscious access or control to any supermarket or store consumers.

It brings this question: How product packing and placement (as in-store factors) and recognition, preferences, and choice task (as out-of-store factors) which will influence the supermarket / store consumer individual decision making process through visual attention. In split-second decision making, the ability to recognize and comprehend a brand of supermarket/ store product can significantly impact preferences. Hence, how the supermarket/store consumer's eye truly sees what whom mind is prepared to influence how much consumption desire to choose to buy the brand's product in short tim decision making process when he/she stays in the shelf location, it has less than ten or more than ten different kinds of brands products or foods to let the visitor to choose in the supermarket or store.

Brand owners and product developers will feel responsibilities to overcome promotion or advertising or communicaton challenge in order to let consumers to know their products are launched on the market. However, it is not until the product reaches the supermarket shelf that has good quality to the effort is judged whether it has how much sale number every day in the supermarket. The judges are the consumers themselves how to make decision quickly through the personal time pressure environment with minor package information processing in the supermarket.

What does it take to be consider an option to influence the consumers‘ minds on visual attention in point-of-purchase decision making ? The supermarket's in-store activities and the consumer personal out-of-store activities will influence how his / her visual attention to the brand of products in the supermarket / store any shelf locations when he/she is walking to pass any shelf locations. So, it seems that any supermarkets or stores brands of products sale number , it has relation to every supermarket or store visitors' visual attention throughout the point to point (shelf to shelf) decision making process in the supermarkets / stores. So, how much does the supermarket's visitors' time spending to obtain attention to the brand of produc? it will have possible to influence the brand of any products' sale number in the supermarket/store. Hence, in this limited timeframe, the consumer enters a decision making process that is in itself influenced by in-store and out-of-store both factors.

I shall explain what is supermarket / store space quality factor, e.g. top level versus floor level to different shelf variable height, weigh , or shelf space location factor as well as the product price elasticity and price-quality relationship to the brand of products both factors to influence every consumer decision making in supermarket/store. The in-store factor is more influential factor to compare out-of-store factor to influence consumers' decision in supermarket. For example, where the shampoo brand products are locating to be put on the shelf , it can influence the point to point behavior of shampoo product habitual buyers. If the buyer habitually chooses the shampoo brand products in the shelf location. Also, if all of the shampoo brand products are moved to another shelf locations to display its different kinds of shampoo products to cause the habitual buyer needs to spend much extra time to find where the another new shelf location is displaying the brand's shampoo products.

In this situation, information processing has a heightened decision making role as the buyer needs to spend much time to find where the brand's displayed shampoo products' shelf location to make non-habitual decision making between options. For habitual decisons, the consumer's visual attention is reduced to measuring visual search. However, when the brands of any shampoo products are moved to another new shelf location to display its different kinds of shampoo products. So, the act of another shelf new location search , it will influence the habitual shampoo buyer's visual attention to consider the brand of any shampoo products which are usually used to wash to his/her hair habitually. When he / she can find the other new brands of shampoo products are displayed on the old shelf displayed location of the brand of shampoo products. Hence, the traditional shelf displayed location to the brand of products, when the brand of products are moved to another new displayed shelf locations. This in-store factors that will influence traditional cosnumers through visual attention concerns to this brand of products more or less.

So, supermarket traditional shelf displayed variable location to the brand of products factor, which will have influence to the traditional consumers' visual attention to do either buying the brand's products or buying another brand's products to replace it, when the traditional consumer feels difficult that he/she needs to spend extra longer time to find whether where is the traditional useful product's displayed shelf location. Then, it will be possible to influence the traditional consumer's traditional purchase decision to the brand's product, and he/she will choose to buy another brand of product to replace when it can be displayed to the shelf location to attract the consumer's visual attention more.

It is one important in-store shelf displayed factor to influence the traditional fast-moving consumer individual purchase decision making behavioral change in any supermarkets or stores when they feel hurry to do personal time pressure consumption decision to make purchase final decision in the point to point counter purchase (the brand's of products are moved from the traditional shelf location visual attention moves to the strange shelf location visual attention) in supermarket time pressure consumption environment.

Hence, in supermarket time pressure consumption environment, in -store and out-of-sore both factors can influence fast-moving consumer individual purchase decision making. The in-store factors can influence product packaging, product placement components as well as the out-store factors can influence choice task, preference and brand recognition components. So, it is common to influence supermarket consumers choose do personal time pressure purchase consumption decision of visual attention purchase behaviors. The different brands' products are displayed to different shelf locations in order to cause shelf displaying products' different decision making effect.

However, instead of shelf displaying location factor, package will also influence consumers' decision making, due to the influence of minute differences in packaging design on visual attention. When, the supermarket consumer feels the brands are not familiar or unfamiliar. Then, he/she will spend more time to evaluate and verify the unfamiliar brands' products whether which one is value to buy in her/his decision making process. He/she will feel visual attention need in order to evaluate in set of brand alternatives to make conscious demand mind cognitive effort by involving working memory. So, if the product's package is attractive, even the consumer is unfamiliar the brand's any product choices which are displayed on the shelf location in the supermarket. The brand's attractive package factor can influence the consumer to raise whom visual attention. Then, the attractive package factor can increase much visual attention chance to many consumers when they are walking to pass through the unfamiliar brand's any products' shelf displaying location considerably. So, it explains when attractive package factor may solve the visual attention problem to fast-moving consumers when they are visiting one strange supermarket to find anywhere unfamiliar brand's products' shelf displaying locations. Because they are the non-traditional consumers to the unfamiliar brand's products, they won't be influenced to choose either buying or not buying the unfamiliar brand's products. When the unfamiliar brand's products are moved to another new shelf displayed location. So, if the unfamiliar brand has attractive package to let the non-traditional consumers feel visual attention when they are passing through the strange shelf displayed location. Then, it can raise purchase chance to the non-traditional consumers target number when they are staying in the strange supermarket. In conclusion, the brand of products' shelf displaying location and package factors may bring much influence to any traditonal or non-traditonal consumer behaviors in supermarket or store time pressure consumption environment.

● What kinds of consumption is most
influenced in preference choice
by time pressure

What kinds of services or products are most influenced to consumer behavioral change by time pressure? Can time pressure factor influence more preference to other factors, such as age, culture, income level, habitual shopping, family or friend relationship etc. factors to influence consumer behavioral choice to these kinds of services or products in consumption market? I shall indicate some kinds of services or products consumption models to explain how time pressure can influence consumers to choose to consume its services or buy its products.

Firstly, for theme park entertainment industry example, has it time pressure to cause any theme park visitors, e.g. Walt Disney entertainment theme park to influence them to feel time pressure to enjoy their emotions to play any entertainment machine facilities and it brings negative emotion to choose the entertainment theme park entertainment consumption activities.

For Walt Disney entetainment theme park example, every visitor needs to pay a fixed ticket fee to enter Disney theme park. So, however, he/she chooses to play how many number of entertainment activities facilities, e.g. only one entertainment playing facility, or more than one entertainment playing facilities. The Disney visitor needs to pay the same ticket fee to enter Disney. So, it will cause th visitors feel unfair , they do not choose to play any entertainment facilities or play only less number of entertainment facilities. Because they need to pay the same ticket price to same to the visitors, who choose to play many entertainment facilities number in Disney. So, it brings this question: Does the Disney visitor feel time pressure when he/she chooses to play many number of entertainment facilities , but he/she will not enjoy to carry on other activities in Disney, e.g. shopping, visiting cinema to watch movies, walking around the whole Disney anywhere to view scene activities. Because US Disney entertainment theme park is very large . It has not only entertainment facilities to attract visitors to play. It has many places are value to visitors to visit or enjoy the other free charge entertainment activities , such as visiting Disney gardens, visiting ocean park, visiting Disney cinema to watch free movies, view scene or seeing free charge ocean animal performance shows , going to Disney shopping centres to shopping, visiting Disney library to read books, visiting Disney ocean park to view different kinds of beautiful fishes non-entertainment machine facility playing activities. All of these activities are value to any Disney visitors to choose to play or visit, instead of entertainment machine facilities activities. So, if one visitor hopes only to spend one day in US Walt Disney entertainment theme park. He/she will feel hurry to choose to play any machine entertainment facilities, or he/she won't choose any machine entertainment facilities to play in Disney because he/she also hopes to play other non-machine entertainment facilities activities, e.g. visiting garden, visiting ocean park, visiting library, visiting cinema to watch free movies, visiting garden to play free charge boats water entertainment activities, watching ocean animal show performance etc. different kinds of entertainment activities, even walking around anywhere fun and excite places in Disney theme park. Hence, the Disney visitor will feel time pressure to choose either playing any kinds of entertainment machine facilities or visiting different places in the whole one day in Disney.

Hence, time pressure factor may influence any one of Disney visitors how to choose any entertainment activities to spedn time in Disney. It will bring this question: Because the Disney ticket price is fixed fee, can the Disney visitor will feel unfair to cause negative emotion, if the Disney visitor feels time pressure to choose to play any kinds of machine entertainment activities or doing other non-machine entertainment activities in the Disney visitor's limited timeframe, during he/she stays in Disney? So, it seems that time pressure psychological factor will may influence some Disney visitors to feel unhappy, negative emotion, when they feel their entertainment activities choices are wrong or doing wring entertainment decision making in his/her limited timeframe. Consequently, time pressure factor will influence some feeling time pressure Disney visitors won't choose to enter Disney again. Hence, time pressure factor can have much influence to theme park visitors‘ behavioral change, instead of whether the entertainment theme park's machine entertainment facilities are attractive or enjoyable playing or how many entertainment facilities are supplied to let visitors to play in the entertainment theme park. So, entertainment theme park service providerd need to consider whether their ticket prices are reasonable to let visitors feel, if they do not want to reduce theme park visitors number seriously.

The another example is restaurant food service industry. Can time pressure influence food consumers to choose the restaurant to eat? Instead of food taste, price, seats available providing, restaurant location, public transportation facilities available etc. factors, which can influence the food consumer individual choice to the restaurant.

Is time pressure another one main factor to influence food consumers choice to the restaurant? In what suitation, food consumers will feel time pressure to influence whose preference restaurant choice? I assume that the restaurant 's price is reasonable, public transportation facility is convenient to catch to go to the restaurant, food taste is acceptable to the food consumer. Although all above these factors are accepted to the food consumer . But when the food consumer feels hurry to hope to find one restaurant to eat and he/she hopes to spend less time to sit down to eat in the restaurant , e.g. less than one hour. Then, the food consumer will compare all the restaurants are near to whose working place or school , if he/she is one student or one working person. Because he/she needs to eat lunch to go to school or go to office to work. So, the restaurant's food taste, price is not the main factor to influence him/her to choose to eat. Otherwise, whether the restaurant needs him/her to spend how long queue time to wait, or/and the restaurant needs how long cooking time to let him/her to eat, the restaurant needs him/her to walk how long time to arrive the restaurant. All of these factors concern " efficient cooking time, queue waiting time serice performance" issues to the restaurant, which are the main evaluation requirements to influence the feeling time pressure food consumer to make decision whether he/she either still ought follow the better food taste, cheap food price factors to be preference decision or he/she ought follow short time queue time waiting or without queue time waiting, fast cooking waiting time factors to be preference restaurant consumption decision.

Hence, it seems that a feeling time pressure food consumer, he/she ought choose the restaurant to eat in preference when it does not need him/her to wait long queue time and wait long cooking time. Otherwise, when the food consumer does not feel hurry to eat, he/she outhgt choose the restaurant, it can provide good taste food, cheap price in preference to eat.

Hence, time pressure personal feeling will influence students or working people food consumers' preference restaurant choice when the restaurant can provide short time queue waiting or without queue waiting and fast cooking time service preference to satisfy their needs.

However , in some situation, time pressure can influence consumers to choose the service, even its price is expensive than other services. For example, public transportation tool choices service. When one passenger has need to find one kind public transportation tool to catch from the place to another destination, but the destination is far away from his/her location. He/she hopes to catch the kind of public transportation tool to arrive the destination about one hour. Although, his/her location has cheap public transportation tools to choose, e.g. bus, train, tram, ferry, underground train. But, he/she feels that all of these public transpotation tools need to spend longer time to compare taxi to arrive the destination. Although, these public transportation tools can be possible to arrive the destination withing one houe and they must charge cheaper fee to compare taxi. But, however the passenge hopes to arrive the destination in the shortest time. The most important influential factor is that the passenger feels personal time pressure to need to arrive the destination fastly and taxi public transportation tool is believed the fast transportation tool to arrive any destination to compare other general public transportation tools , when it has no traffic jam external environment factor influence. So, time pressure factor will influence passenger to choose taxi transportation tool in preference. Also, it seems that when the place often has many time pressure passengers are living. Then, the place's taxi business will be possible better than other locations. Hence, it implies that time pressure factor will bring need or demand number to be increased to some services.

Time pressure also influences how consumers choose to buy the kind of product, when he/she feels that the kind of product will be old fashin or it is not popular to use in society. For example, computer product, the traditional desktop large heavy weight computers will be possible to be replaced to use at home or office or any building places. Due to the laptop small light weight computers , it can be brought to anywhere by the users easily, even it can be brought to catch public transportation tool to use, it can be brought to restaurant, library, shopping centre etc. different public places to use conveniently. Due to some working people feel hurry to use computer to do their tasks, e.g. typing one document in short time. If they are not working in office and they have no computer on hand. They will worry about that they can not finish their tasks to give their bosses in limited time on the working day.

Hence, laptop computer will be one good chocie of task tool for busy working people when they need to often to use computer to finish urgent tasks in any time. Hence, it seems that the feeling time pressure working people will choose laptop computer in preference more than desktop traditional computer working tool. Due to the feeling time pressure workers, they feel that they can not finish their daily tasks in office. So, they will feel to need to use laptop computer task tool to help them to do office tasks . When they are catching transportation tool to go home or office time or lunch time , or holiday time. So, laptop computer product is more popular to time pressure working people target consumers.

Laptop computer products can also increase the feeling time pressure student consumers‘ needs. Because when one students feel home time is not enough to use computer to do their homeworkers at homes. When some students finish all lessons in schools and they need to catch public transportation tools to go home, in this catching public transportation time, they will be possible to hope to use one laptop computer to do their homeworks. So, one student who often feels time pressure to do whose homeworks, he will feel need to buy one laptop to carry it to anywhere, e.g. library, garden, school etc. different places. Then, he/she can do whom housework at any places in any time conveniently. Hence, it seems that their laptop computer products will be time pressure consumers' preference task tool.

In conclusion, the different factors influence consumer behaviors. Time pressure factor may be one main factor to influence consumers to choose to buy the kind of product or consume the kind of service in preference. So, when th consumer feels time presure to influence him/her to do preference choice to consume the kind of service of buy the kind of product. It is possible to occur to influence he/she does irrational economic choice decision. Hence, time pressure factor can being positive or negative both consumption emotion to some kinds of services or products . Hence, the increasing or decreasing number of consumers to some kinds of products or services, it has absolute relationship between of them. So, any product sellers or service providers can not neglect the importance of how time pressure factor influences consumer behavior in our nowadays society.

- Time pressure impacts consumer behavioral effect

I shall indicate cases to explain that how time pressure environment factor impacts consumer behavior as well as what effects will be brought by time pressure consumer behavioral cause. Instead of above discussions concern how customer personal time pressure psychological factor influence, whether hoe time pressure environment factor will also influence consumer behavior. What are the difference between time pressure environment factor and time pressure consumer personal psychological factor? I shall explain as below:

Firstly, the impact of life satisfaction is caused by time pressure on consumers responses. Can effective advertising can impact of life satisfaction when the consumer feels need to buy the kind of product in any time pressure environment? Can effective advertising bring direct impact on sales when the consumer feels need to buy the kind of product in time pressure environment? Effective advertising may being advantages, includes customers feel easy to accept of price increases, favorable publicity, and reshaping market segmentation.

However, when the customer feels need life satisfaction in time pressure lif environment. The time pressure life environment ought impact on the consumer responses on advertising. Hence, when the consumer needs to live in the time pressure life environment. The over-commercialization of advertising ought impact the consumer chooses to buy the brand of product, when the seller has attractive advertising to bring purchase incentives to influence consumption desire to the time pressure environment influential consumer. For example, when the summer season will change to winter season, the ice cream consumers begins to feel weather will change to cold weather. Because many people feel more colf in the beginning. This is seasonable time pressure environment feeling, it may influence many ice-cream likers feel ice-cream may be possible shortage in hot weather or summer season, due to many ice-creams will be bought in summer weather to cause supermarkets in possible. So, if the brand ice-cream can make attractive advertisement to persuade ice-incream number will be reduced in the coming winter season beginning. So, it may influence many ice-cream likers choose to buy this brand's ice-cream in preference in summer. Because they feel fear none of any this brand's ice-creams can be sold in supermarkets in summer. Because they feel this brand's ice-cream , it's problem to let they can buy any different kinds of ice-cream taste to eat from any supermarkets in summer season. Hence, it explains why effective or attractive advertising may increase sale number, when consumers feel the brand's product number will be shortage or reduced from the seasonal time pressure external environment factor influence.

Secondly, I shall discuss what is the relationship between the effects of product popularity and time pressure on consumer responses? When a brand is popular to let many customers to familiarize in society. Does it increase time pressure to influence consumers choose in preference? Time pressure remaining to product popularity concerns how much sale number is raised to persuade consumers to choose to buy a preference for ecommerce online shopping. It seems to be one time pressure online sale environment. The effects of the ecommerce online shopping environment has relationship beteen pressure and product popularity on perceived risk and purchase intention.

In ecommerce online sale environment time pressure is operationized at the time remaining for consumers to sign up the online seller' website and property popularity is operationlized to the number of products already sold at the moment when consumers visit the web page. Hence, when on online consumer has intention to buy any products from internet. He/she will attempt to type the product name, then he/she will find some webpages which can provide the different brands of product photos, their prices informations to let the consumer to compare whether which brand of product price is more reasonable, better quality , good product image from the web pages' advertisement information to let him/her to evaluate. Hence, any product web page will influence how every online custmer feeling is good or bad to the web page's any brands of products. If the consumer feel the web page has many high product popularity indicators, it may bring a high consumption desire to let the online cusomer to evaluate the web page all prodocts in order to compare which brand of product is the best to choose to buy in time webpage view pressure consumption environment. Otherwise, if the consumer feels the web page has high product popularity indicator , it may bring a less consumption desire to let the online consumer to evaluate any of the webpage products to choose to buy. So, online webpage advertising information will be one time pressure online ecommerce consumption environment.

I assume that online shopping consumers won't like to stay to view on any webpage long time. It is possible that they choose to click more web pages to hope to find more different familiar and unfamiliar both brands of products informations in order to make more accurate comparison and evaluation from more different kinds of brands of products in order to make the most accurate online shopping decision. Hence, any brands of products online webpage information will be one time pressure limited sale environment to consumers feel that they need to make the most accurate online purchase decision in short time. Moreover, it seems that if the brand of products which can be showed on the popular product webpage, the it will have much sale chance to let online purchasers familiarize in order to increase sale opportunity more easily.

Finally, I shall explain what is the meaning of external time pressure consumption environment is the long time queue waiting consumption environment. I shall explain how to achieve one simplistic queueing system to solve long time queue waiting problem to bring consumers' negative emotion influence to choose to consume the service or buy the product in preference.

For entertainment service example, e.g. queueing at the cinema counter to buy one ticket to watch the movie , or queueing at the music hall to buy one ticket to listen the music performance show activities. The audiences' ticket purchase aims to sit down in the cinema or music hall to enjoy to listen and see pretty music performance or watch the attractive movie comfortable within one to two hours entertainment time. If the movie or music performance show is attractive, the cinema or music hall will have many audiences accept to spend long time to queue to buy the ticket. However, if the cinema ot music hall needs audience consumers to queue long time to buy the ticket, e.g. one houe , even more than one houe queueing time to wait to buy the ticket to watch the movie or listen the music performance show. Then, the long time queue waiting problem will be possible to cause a lot audiences number to be reduced, because they feel that they need to spend much time pressure to queue to by the ticket to listen the music performance show or watch the movie.

However, of these unacceptable too long queue time audiences can have another/ other cinema(s), music hall(s) to buy the same price , even more low price of movie ticket or music performance show ticket in short time. Then, they must leave the present cinema queue and go to the another cinema or music hall to buy ticket to watch the same movie or listen the same music performance show. So, long time queue is one external time pressure environment to influence consumer's preference choice to the service provider, when they feel it has another service provider does not need them or these audiences need to spend same long time queue time to wait to buy the ticket in order to enjoy the service, e.g. listening music performance show, watching movie.

Hence, in a high time pressure queue situation where decision makers, e.g. audiences have less time than needed (or perceived needed). It is very likely that they feel the queue waiting time stress of copying with themselves queue waiting time maximum limitation. So, if the movie ticket purchase audience feels that he/she will need to spend more than half hour to queue and half hour is himself/herself the maximum acceptable queue time level. So, his/her queue long time pressur negative emotion feeling will influence him/her to leave the cinema to choose another cinema. He/ she feels that ir does not need him/her to queue more than half hour in order to buy the ticket to watch the same movie in the another cinema, he/she can feel more comfortable to watch the movie. So, long time queue will influence some audiences choose aother service provider to replace it in possible short time, when they feel waiting in a queue is irritating, frustrating and hence costly.

What is a simplistic queueing system and how it can solve above queue problem. For a grocery store queueing counter case example, for one Apply brand computer shop example, the day's most busy queue time , there are about between fifty and hundred Apply brand potential computer buyers numbers every hour in the day. They need to queue to enquire the salespeople concern to any useful opinions to let them to know in order to make purchase decisions. But, the Apple brand computer shop lacks enough salespeople to answer their enquiries concern any computer purchase challenges. Every computer enquiry potential purchaser needs to spend at least half hour , even more time to queue to wait the salesperson to answer his/her enquiry in the counter queueing line. Hence, the feeling long time queue enquiry waiting consumers will feel time pressure to queue. Then, they will choose to leave the Apple brand computer shop's counter queue line. Consequently, the Apple brand computer will lose many potential computer buyers on the busy day.

The most simple solution is that it can increase the salespeople number in the most busy enquiry time every day. Hence, when every computer potential enquiry customer can contact every salesperson to listen whom opinion concerns his/her any computer enquiry issues in order to let he/she feels that they every one can provide excellent sale service computer issues enquiry explanation performance to satisfy his/her enquiry need to let himself/herself to feel in the short enquiry time. Due to they do not need to spend long queue time to wait every salesperson's feedback or opinion to solve their enquiries in the computer shop. Because they do not feel presure to spend long time to queue to wait the computer shops's every salesperson's opinion. So, they will raise satisfactory feeling to thie Apple computer shop's every salesperson individual sale enquiry service performance.

Consequently, the day's computer sale number will be possible to raise after the salespeople can spend much time to solve their enquiries effectively and efficiently.

● The reasons cause consumers feel
time pressure

What factors can cause consumers feel time pressure to but the product in the personal time limited dominated consumption environment? It is one interesting question: Why does the consumer feel time pressure to make short time purchase decision making? I shall indicate some cases to explain this possibility as below:

First, I shall indicate household purchaser time pressure consumption behavior. Consumer house buyer behavior, some house buyer will feel personal time pressure to choose the different houses to make house purchase decision in short time. For example, if the house developer has a 30% discount house price to sell only in the short three months. So, after this three months, all house purchaser will need to pay the original house price. If the house developer's houses prices are between US doller one million to two million every house. For one million house price after

30% discount , the house buyer only needs to pay seventy million. For two million house price after 30 % discount, the house buyer only needs to pay one hundred and fourty million. So, expensive product's financing factor will influence the buyer's consumption time pressure, such as the house discount price case, due to the house developer's houses prices are very expensive. However, if any house buyers can make decisin to buy its houses in three months. Then, they can pay les 30% of the houses prices. Such as the original price one million house, the house buyer can pay less thirty million amount or the original price two million houses prices. The house buyer can pay less sixty million amount. So, the large discount financing amount may be attractive purchase method to influence many house buyers feel time pressure to decide whether they ought choose to buy the property developer's houses in these three months. It is one short term cheap house financing price to let many house buyers feel time pressure to make house purchase decision from this house developer in these three months . Hence, short term high discount price to expensive product financing factor will influence consumers feel it is right time to make pressure consumption decision.

Hence, such as this three months house discount price case, when the property buyer gain this property developer's knowledge of three months house discount price message. This sudden three months house discount price message will be one attractive knowledge of factor to impact the potential property buyers' house purchase desires to be raised in three months time pressure house purchase consumption environment. So, it is one feeling sudden time pressure consumption desire good example for this three monts large discount attractive houes price to influence house buyers to make house purchase decision from the house developer in these three months. Consequently, house developer will have possible to raise the large house sale number , if this 30 % house discount price can let many property buyers feel it is one worth purchase price in these three months. So, they will consider that they can not pay less 30% discount price to buy this house developer's any houses after three months. So they need to make house purchase decision in these three months short term time pressure house consumption market for this property developer.

So, this time pressure financing advantage will only bring benefit to this property developer, this time pressure financing advantage won't bring benefit to other property developers, because all property buyers feel need to make property purchase decision in these three months suddenly, due to this property developer can provide a special 30 discount price to any property final decision making to choose to buy its houses in these three months temporary short time. It seems that three months short time can cause final house purchase choice time pressure to any potential property buyers. They expect to gain high discount price to buy any expensive houses. So, these expenaive house potential buyers will feel need to make final expensive house purchase decision to choose to buy this property developer's expensive houses in these final three months perios. So, time pressure can occur in any short period, when the seller can provide any special sale promotion to persuade consumers to feel need to make sudden time pressure that purchase decision is they hope to earn special sale promotion consumption in the short limited sale perios for the seller.

Hence, consumer personal time pressure feeling, it can be predictive to any time occurrence pychological consumption, feeling, such as the property developer's sudden high per cent discount price to expensive house less dinancing burden factor to influence the expensive house buyers feel that whether they ought do choice house purchase decision in these short term three months , because the house developer's unpredictive and sudden attractive expensive houses reducing prices strategy. So, this property developer's short term three months high house discount price time pressure consumption strategy may persuade or attract , even encourage many potential expensive house buyers choose to spend lesser amount to buy this property developer's discount houses, either is paid by house mortgage bank loan lending payment method or installment payment method or on-time all payment method. So, the different house payment choice buyers will be influenced to make immediate property purchase decision in these three months time pressure period from this property developer's expensive discounted house number influence.

However, in this house market time pressure consumption environment, the property developer's expensive house supply number may also have influential effort to excite the expensive house buyers' house purchase consumption desires, for example, if the other expensive house property developers' between US one million and US two million of every property price's these houses in the country's property marker totel suppy number is one thousand property unit number. The potential property buyers , they plan to buy these amounts of expensive houses , the property needers estimate three thousand buyers number at least. Hence, it seems that these expensive house buyers' demand id more than three times to expensive property supply number.

Moreover, the other property developer's expensive property developers ' expensive house prices have no any discount in this three months periods, and some property developers' expensive house prices tend to increase 1 to 10 per cent in these three months period. Hence if the property developer can supply at least three thousand property units number between US one million and US two million sale price and all of these expensive houses are reduced 30 per cetnt discount to sell in these three months .

Consequently, it is possible to persuade all estimated three thousand expensive house potential buyers choose to buy this property developer's houses in these three months in possible. So, it explain that why this property developer's expensive discounted house supply number will influence these property buyers' preference choice. If this property developer has only one thousand expensive houses to be supplied by discounted 30% sale price. Then, it will cause shortage of expensive houses to satisfy these three thousand expensive house buyer estimated number in the country in three month discount sale promotion period.

Consequently, this property developer will lose two thousand these prices of expensive house potential buyers number in all these three months discounted sala period . I assume that all these three thousand expensive house property buyers will be influenced to make choice to buy its all dicounted expensive houses in these three month time pressure discounted sale period. So, it needs to do data gather concerns how many of thee expensive house potential house buyers number in its country in order to avoid discounted expensive houses supply number to cause shortage supply challenges and bring these expensive house potential buyers lose number in these three months period.

In conclusion, it explains why that supply number will influence this property developer's sale number in these three months sale period. Consequently, time pressure sale strategy ans supply number has close relationship to influence the seller's sale number in the time pressure sale period.

Secondly, I shall discuss how does environment time pressure factor influences consumer behavior? Does time pressure influence consumer donating behavior? I assume that external environment time pressure factor can influence consumer changes whom original purchase decision making. What circumstance's time can influence consumer individual to feel time pressure to consume. For example, when the consumer expects have one hour to choose whether which brand of product to buy among the different kinds of products. The circumstance is changed suddenly. It influences the consumers feel that they has only 10 minutes to make the final purchse decision.

Why does the consumer feel enough brand of product? What external circumstance factors influence he/she feels only 10 minutes time to make the final purchase decision suddenly? For travel fair time limited external environment influential pressure travelling consumption case example, the international travel fair can indicate that time limited pressure has positive significant influence on traveller perceived value and purchase intention in short time. In addition, perceived value is served as a mediating factor between the relationship of time limited pressure and feeling travelling entertainment purchase intention to the travel fair visitors. It has a beneficial reference for planning a travelling show or fair marketing strategy.

One attractive travelling fair/show can promote the country's different attractive travelling destinations to let the travellinf show's visitors to know. It can particularly influence the visitors' long time travelling planning , it can be shorten be short time travelling planning, e.g. after one year's travelling planning can be influenced to make immediate focused on choosing the country's travelling decision if he/she feels the country has more attractive travelling destinations, he/she prefers to go to travel in short time, e.g. within 6 months . So, when the travelling exhibition fair/ show can provide the country's beautiful scene photos to let the visitors to view. Then, it will bring effective time pressure feeling to let some travelling visitos feel travelling needs immediately in the travelling exhibition show/ fair . This travelling exhibition show/fair can bring the time limited pressure benefit. It is as an external environment factor that can influence the travelling visitors' travelling desires to be raised , when they can view many benefitical scene photos of the country' different undiscovered travelling destination . Then, it can increase their travelling desires to the country in possible.

I shall explain why travelling exhibition show/fair can play an important role in travelling consumer perceived quality and travelling country destination choice decision making to influence travelling visitors feel time limited pressure. However, perceived value has been show to be a value has been shown to be a value of perceived quality and perceived sacrifice to cause travelling visitors feel more interesting to choose to travel the country when they can view the attractive beautiful scence photos in the travelling exhibition show/fair.

A successful travelling exhibition show/fair can bring time limited process increases , the travelling visitors pay more attention to key travelling destination features and positive travelling information from the scene photos and travelling destinations introduction. So , the country's attractive travelling destinations scene photos and clear travelling introduction to different destinations information will be important message to let the different countries' travelling visitors to know when they spend a limited time to enter the travelling exhibition show/fair to view the different scene photos . If the travelling visitor feel very satisfied to the country's travelling exhibition show/fair. Then, this travelling exhibition excite whom travelling interest to choose to go to the country to travell in short time, when the travelling visitors are influenced to feel the country has many beautiful destinations where they feel have travelling interest in the limited time pressure travelling exhibition show/fair environment. If the travelling exhibition show/fair needs they to pay enter fee and it has only two hours or less time to premit to stay in the travelling exhibition show/fair.

Hence, if the time pressure limited travelling exhibition show/fair can let the travelling visitors feel attractive and enjoyable view feeling when they look every the country's any scene beautiful photos and indication how to the different travelling destinations and explains why the country's travelling places are value travelling destinations to let the exhibition visitors to know, when they do not know or discover these any one of value travelling places in the country before. Then, this limited time staying travelling exhibition show/fair will bring positive time pressure to influence some travelling visitors feel interesting to visit the country's inknown or undiscovery travelling destinations in short time. So, all attractive travelling exhibition shows/fairs are one external environment time limited positive pressure factor to excite some travelling visitors' travelling desires in short time in possible.

Instead of travelling exhibition show/fair can bring external environment positive limited time positive pressure to excite travelling visitors' travelling consumption desires, the another external environment positive limited time positive pressure case is that mobile coupons of limited mobile phone sale number or discount mobile phone call payment plan in short time case. How and why mobile coupons can excite any mobile consumption and/ or mobile phone call user choice to the mobile phone sale company or mobile

phone call service provider.
An effective mobile plane useful limited time beneficial purchase strategy can encourage some mobile phone consumers to choose to use the brand mobile useful phone call service plan immedicately. if the mobile phone call service plan is attractive to the mobile phone call consumer . For example, dynamic discounts strategies are used by marketers to send scaraity message which lead to higher consumers' mobile phone purchase intention. An utility increasing discount straregy provides mobile phone call users with an increasing discount over time (e.g. 30% discount for in-store consumption for 30 minutes, after which the discount increases to 40 % , an utility discount strategy provides the same discounts for mobile phone call users over a specific promotional period (e.g. 40% discount from 9AM to 5 PM) phone call using time. An utility decreasing discount strategy offers mobile phone call users with a decreasing discount over time (e.g. 40% discount for in -store consumption for 10 minutes, after which the discount decreases to 30%).
However, these three different discount strategies for bargaining have different impacts on outcomes. However, they have same influences to lead mobile phone call users feel time pressure to do choose whether this mobile phone call using plan is suitable. If the mobile phone call user feels this mobile phone call using plan is suitable to use, then this mobil coupon promotion strategy can influence mobile phone user feels limited time pressure to persuade him/her to choose to use its mobile phone call service under different time limitation, quantity limitation and discount strategies on the mobile phone user's mobile phone call plan using intention.
Furthermore, I hypothesize that the brand of mobile phone quantity, limited scarcity message that gives a perception that the brand of any kinds of mobile phones are limited for purchase, it will have a positive impact on mobilt phone consumers‘ perceived value of mobile products, leading to a greater tendancy to make mobile phone purchase decision immediately. Hence, mobile coupon is one type of price-incentive promotion. In various price incentives, discount strategy is a mode of price negotiation between the mobile product conumer and the merchant, such as the mobile phone seller , mobile phone call user and mobile phone call service provider.
However, mobile coupons offer discount under a time constraint to induce perceived scarcity. Scarce commodities are more attractive than those with plenty inventory due to the speciality and uniqueness of the former perceived by the consumer. However, scarcity has both forms. They incluce

quantity scaracity can let consumers feel need to buy the product in short time. Otherwise, due to stock shortage or low inventory to influence they can not brought the kind of product. Time scarcity means products are for sale only for a designated

● May time dominate consumption
final purchase decision making

Whether can time limited pressure dominate consumer individual to make more rational purchase decision? Can the consumer make more rational decision , when he/she has enough time to make final purchase decision? I shall explain why and how the consumer can make more rational decision when he/she has enough time as well as I shall explain that without time pressure environment. It may dominate consumers to make more rational or more accurate decision making.

I assume that it is the final time limited pressure day to nee the consumer to spend more nervous do time final purchase decision among the different kinds of similar products choices, e.g. air conditions . If the consumer decides that the day is the final purchase decisin to choose to buy one air conditin among these different brands of similar air conditions in the super store. So, if on the that day, he/she can not make any final decisin to choose which brand of air condition to buy on that final consumption day in the super store when the super store visitor sees the final air condition consumption day advertisement in this year in this super store . Then, he/ she won't buy any air condition again if he/she can not buy on that day in this super store.

The another time dominates immediate purchase behavior is that I assume that one common air condition can not be bought in short time later if all air condition consumers can not make decision to buy any air condition in this super store. So, his/her personal time limited pressure can dominate whose final or condition purchase decision in this super store on that day. If the store has many different brands of air conditions to lead him/her to spend long time to compare which is th best worth to buy in this super store. Then, it will let him/her to feel difficult to make the air condition final purchase decision in the store on that day. Otherwise, if the super store has less different brands of air conditions to need him/her to spend less time to compare which is the best worth to buy in the store. Then, he/she may make the final air conditin purchase decision making more easily on that day.

So, the final air condition purchase day of the super store, the super store's air condition final day's time can dominate the air condition buyer to make air condition purchase decision immediately. Due to he/she feels that all of these day brands air conditions can not bought from this super store after that day. So, he/she needs to make the air condition purchase decision making in this super store on that final air condition purchase day in this year. Because it is the final air condition purchase day in this super store of all sir conditions products. If he/she can not make the choice to buy any one brand of air condition in this store. Then, it is possible that he/she will lose this store's final cheap price air condition purchase benefits. However, if this super store has too many brands of air conditions need him/her to choose. It will cause him/her to spend more time to choose. Consequently, it will cause he/she feels difficult to compare which brand of air condition is the best and he / she does not choose to buy any one in this super store.
Hence, this super store ought have less number different brands of air conditions to let every air condition consumer to choose in order to let they can make final air condition purcahse decision on this air condition cheap price purchase final day. So, less different number brands of air conditions will dominate the consumers to spend less time to make purchase decision immediately and easily on that final sale day in this super store. Hence, it seems that the super store's final air conditions sold day time will dominate many air condition visitors to make purchase decision when they visit this super store in summer season on that day in this super store. Because all this super store's air condition consumers do not expect that they can not buy the best quality of air conditin in this super store final sold day , due to air condition stocks number shorten challenge is not supplied enough on that final cheap purchase day in this super store. Consequently, that time pressure will increase to influence them to make the final air condition purchase decision in the final sold day' s short time, before this super store closing time on that day. Their time pressure feeling comes from the super store 's air condition number shortage supply in possibility. It will dominate them to make the final air condition purchase decision in this super store in short time.
The anothe time dominates immediate purchase behavior case is that I assume that one common picture painter(actor), he finds one architect to help him to build one house. The architect only needs to folloe his house picture to build one house. The common picture painter tells him that he will give him building expenditure and building profit after he helps him

to build the house profit after he helps him to build the house successfully. After six months, the architect made one decision, he did not demand the famous picture painter paid him for the building service fee. But, he needed him give the house picture to him to replace the building service fee. Because the picture painter feels that he didn't need to pay the building service fee to him to buy the architect's building service in these six months building time. Hence, he accepted his offer to give his common house picture to the architect for his reward.

I assume that this six months time dominate the architect to make the final building service fee decision either acceptance the common picture painter customer's building service fee or acceptance his common house picture replaces the building service fee. However, the architect believes that this common house picture can have higher selling price to compare his building service fee income. Consequently, I assume that his evaluation is right, this house picture selling price is more than three times to compare his past six months's building service income. So, it proved that his choice is right, because he could earn more than three times of his building service income after he decided to accept the common picture painter's this house picture to attempt to sell it in the picture auction market. It seems that this six months long house building time can dominate these both buyer and seller's purchase and selling behaviors, such as this picture painter and this architect. When the architect has this six months enough time to let the picture painter to change his building service offer decision from building service fee payment to his common house picture offer exchange. This architect can achieve his intention to let him to accept his free house picture sold product exchange offer more easily. Otherwise, if the architect can not need six months to build this house, he only needs three months or less time to build this house, then it is possible that the picture painter won't accept his this house picture offer to replace his building service fee easily. If he considers that whether his this house picture's selling price has possible to sell higher price to compare this building service fee for this house picture. He will choose to sell this house picture himself. Hence, due to the picture painter can not sell this house picture in this past six months. So, in this six months period, the house painter can not sell this house picture in picture auction market. This six months period can dominate his low market worth selling feeling to this house picture as well as it can influence him to make this house picture exchange decision to replace his house service fee.

The picture painter will ask himself, ought the house picture painter need to wait how long time to sell this picture in auction market, because he does not know whether the architect needs how long time to build this house? So, this house building time can dominate the picture painter's acceptance of the architect's this free house picture product exchange offer, which is easier acceptance or difficult acceptance . In this six month' house building period between the architect service provider and the picture painter house buyer. Hence,the house building time can dominate the house building provider and the picture painter's house building buyer both's house picture free exchange purchase change behavioral choice between of them influentially.

The another time dominates consumption behavior case is that time rich or time poor factor, e.g. one fast food famous restaurant , its success is not only due to its fast food good taste factor, its restaurant location whether is close to the time poor people's offices, it is one main factor. Because this fast food famous restaurant only choose to build its restaurants to close to offices in any large cities in different countries. Hence, the franchisees need to pay expensive franchise loyalty income to buy its franchise in order to it can supply fast foods to the franchisees to sell, but they also need to pay expensive rent to this fast food franchiser, due to their fast food restaurant locations has been chose to locate in the main cities in different countries from the fast food famous restaurant's location decision. Hence, whether long or short time fast restaurant rent period to the franchisees , which can dominate the fast food restaurants's royalty and rent income. For example, if one fast food franchisee only sign one year contract to buy the fast food franchisor's loyalty to help it to sell its fast foods only one year, because it does not ensure how many fast food consumers will choose to buy these fast foods to eat, due to its price is decided by the fast food franchisor. If the cities have other fast food restaurants to let them to choose, they may find other fast food restaurants to replace it to eat fast foods very easily. If this fast good restaurant is not the most famous and it operates only short time. So, it can not earn more fast food franchisees' confidence to accept to pay long time rent to operate its fast food restaurants in cities and pay long time royalty fee to it. Otherwise, if the fast food restaurant had operated its restaurant for a long time period to raise its fast food loyalty's to let many different countries' fast food eaters to familiarize or acknowledg its fast food brand in popular. So, long fast food opersation time can confirm that it has many fast food eaters, they prefer to choose to eat its fast foods. It can increase the franchisees' confidence to choose to rent its fast food restaurants and pay royalty to it in preference. Hence, the fast food franchisor's restaurant operation time whether it is long or short time, this franchisor's fast food restaurant operating time pressure factor will dominate the fast food franchisees‘ choices to decide to pay how long rent sand franchise royalty income to rent its restaurant to do the franchisee's fast food business in the cities locations in different countries. So, it seems that the fast food franchisor's business operation time can dominate the frahchisees' choice.

In special , in fast food industry, time rich and time poor consumers behavior will dominate their fast food choices. Time rich people feel they have enough or too much time when time poor people feel time is a major constraint in their daily life. The explansion of the fast food business, and the increase eatting of fast food are indicators of this trend. At the same time, shorter working hours increased wealth and less pressure on domestic rountines have opened up new segments of leisure consumption. But, " free time" in certain areas has not for many people, lead to an increases feeling of time richness.

So, it explains that why many fast food consumers who feel not enough time to work daily. They are time poor working people usually. So, instead of fast food taste factor influences consumer number. The people who feel time rich or poor, e.g. employmet rich or poor lunch time to the employee, it will dominate the employee chooses to go to fast food restaurant in preference. So, the fast food restaurant can supply rich time to let them to eat lunch in short time, if the employee has less time to eat lunch or more tasks need hime to do on that day afternoon. Hence, feeling time rich or poor to the people factor, which will dominate some consumers‘ choices to some kinds of businesses, such as fast food industry, or for public transportation tool choice case example, one time poor passenger feels need to go to the destination in short time. The time poor passenger will prefer to choose taxi in preference, then it is possible train or underground train, next it is tram, fainally, it is bus or ferry public transportion tool choices. Otherwise, for one time rich passenger, he has more time to go to the destinaton. The time rich passenger will prefer to choose the cheap public transportation tool , such as bus, ferry, underground train, ferry, train. The final choice is taxi. So, passenger's time pressure will influence whose public transportation tool choice.

- Time pressure dominiates consumer psychological factor

What are the factors of time pressure dominate consumer purchcase psychological behaviors? How any why do this time pressure psychological factors dominate consumer behaviors? It is possible that time pressure can dominate consumer mind and behavior either choose to buy the product/ consume the service or not buy the product/consume the service. Every consumer's final purchase decision, he/she is influenced how to make by himself/herself personal psychological limited time pressure . It means that he/she will have one time maximum standard to demand himself/herself to make the final purchase decision in whose individual psychological time standard (the consumer's individual psychological limited consumption time). So, it seems that ever consumer's final decision how he/she chooses to buy the product or consume the service, his/her consumption behavior will be dominated by whose psychological time limited consumption pressure.

So, time pressure issue seems evolutionary psychology, it looks at how consumer behavior has beed affected by psychological adjustments during time pressure evoluation. It seeks to identify which consumer psychological traits are evolved through adaptations, e.g. time pressure consumption adaptations to choose the final purchase decision in the final time limited consumption pressure environment, e.g. the consumer expects this day is the final day to choose to buy what kinds of the product. If he/she can't make final purchase decisin on the day, he/she will choose to buy the kind of product later, even he/she does not choose to buy the kind of product in the first or again, that is the products of natural selection, or the supermaket visitor case, he expects to choose which kind of food to eat within final 15 minutes, if he/she can't make the final decision to buy what kind of food to eat within final 15 minutes in this supermarket , or the restaurant eatting consumer case, he is queueing to wait to enter the restaurant to eat. He/ she expects the final queue waiting time is 15 minutes maximum. If after this 15 minutes, he/she can not be permited to enter this restaurant, then he/she will choose to leave this restaurant and he/she will find another restaurant to replace it. So, it seems that any consumer will have himself/ herself consumption limited stardard time to decide whether he/she ought choose to buy any products or consume any services in any consumption environment.

Hence, the cause of consumption time pressure dominates consumer behavior, it is based on these hypothesis: Every consumer has demand characteristic and time pressure can dominate how he/she make final decision to buy or not buy any product or consume any service as well as any consumer needs have time pressure consumption demand because he/she does not expect to epend more time to choose what kinds of products to buy or what kinds of services to consume. He/she expects to make purchase or consumption final decision in short time.

IN fact, consumers will be encoded to influence how they make final purchase decision. There are three main ways in which product information can be encoded. They include: Visual (product picture) ; for example, the conumer stores the memory by visualizing it as on product image. Aconstic (sound); here the consumer stores the information as a sound , this explains why some consumers sometimes get the brand name(words) that sound the same mixed up when they try to remember them. Semantic (meaning); here the object is stored in terms of what it means rather than as an image or sound, e.g. when the brand of toys can let many children feel fun to play. Then, when many parents feel familiar to the toy brand, they must remember this toy brand company is selling any kinds of toys to let children to play. So, famous brand can let consumers familiarize what products that it is selling. Such as the toy brand company can let parents feel its toys are fun to let their children to play. All these sensory information can dominate consumers make final choice purchase behavior to buy its product or consume its service in preference in any time limited pressure environment, if the brand can give positive information memory to let many customers to remember.

So, it seems that consumers are dominated to choose which kinds of products to buy or which kinds of services to consume by positive or negative emotion, time pressure in any consumption environment immediately. It is one time pressure consumption environment theory factor, it can influence consumer behavior is changed in any consumption environment time. Consequently, it explains that why time pressure can dominate consumer behaviors in possible. Also, any product seller or service provider needs to consider how to manage consumption time process to be longer to cause its consumers doe not choose to buy its product or consume its service consequently.

● Methods avoid consumers
feel time pressure

In business society, it seems that any consumers will feel time pressure to

cause their purchase decision making process changes in any consumption suitations, when they feel time pressure either by themselves or third parties influence, e.g. not buying any thing, not consuming any service, irrational making consumption final decision etc. consumption behaviors. How to reduce their time pressure to avoid they do above consumption behaviors. I shall indicate some consumption suitations to explain how to avoid their reducing consumption , due to time pressure factor influences as below:

Firstly, I shall indicate supermarket consumption environment example. In general, supermarket visitors will expect to spend less time to visit any supermarkets to make choice to biy any foods. They will stay short time when they expect to buy less foods, even, they will stay more short time when they expect to buy more less foods in any supermarkets. So, any supermarkets will need to calculate their clients' limited time pressure how to influence their foods consumption number. If the supermarket visitor expects to spend maximum 20 minutes to buy any foods in the supermarket. Then, he may choose some different kinds of foods to buy, e.g. icecream, fruit, bread, jam, fish etc. different kinds of foods, Otherwise, if the another supermarket visot expects to spend maximum 10 minutes to buy any foods in the supermarket. Then, he may choose less different kinds of foods to compare the first one, e.g. fish, jam, icecream only or bread, fruit , jam only. So, the second one supermarket visitor will buy less different kinds of foods, because he expects to spend 10 minutes maximum , his shopping spending time is less 10 minutes to compare the first one supermarket visitor. Because different supermarket visitor personal time pressure will limit him/her to choose more or less different kinds of foods to buy. However, time pressure will not influence every kind of foods number because every kind of food purchase number will not be influenced to buy more or less , due to the supermarket visitor personal time pressure variable factor influences his/her foods purchase number. Otherwise, the different kinds of food choice will be influenced to choose to either buy or not buy , due to every supermarket visitor personal time pressure is different.

Hence, supermarkets can focus on how to avoid any kinds of food purchase choice loses , due to supermarket consumer personal time pressure influences. In fact, in supermarket every shelf, it usually has many different brands of every kind of foods to let supermarket visitors to choose to buy. For example,the kind of jam food number has many brands are placed on shelf to let them to choose, e.g. there are more than 10 different brands of jam food are placed on one shelf. It will bring one choice problem. IF one supermarket visitor expects to choose one brand of jam within 5 minute, then he finds the shelf has more than 10 different brands of jam are placed on the shelf. Then he will feel time pressure to cause difficulty to choose the best brand of jam to buy from these 10 brands of jam. It will bring the negative emotion if he feels that all of these 10 brands of jam taste and price has no more difference. Consequently, these 10 brands of jam choice will cause he can not make the final jam purchase decision within this 5 minutes individual time limited. Anyway, if there are only 5 brands of jam are placed on this shelf, then the 5 minutes time limited consumer will has less brands of jam choices, it will influence him to do more easy choice to buy one kind of brand jam food from the shelf. It is one limited time pressure of psychological choice factor to influence any consumers feel to do any brand of food choice more easy in short time. Hence, I recommend supermarket shelf ought place every kind of food brand maximum to 5 brands , it is the best food brand number to every supermarket's shelves to let any consumers to choose different kinds of foods to make the easy food choice way in supermarket food market.

So, in super store market, it is similar to supermaket market. Super stores' main products are cloths, shoes, bags, stationarys, electronic products, e.g. fans, air conditions, televisons, radios, warmers, washing machines, dry machines, computers etc. However, super store visitors will like to spend more time to stay in any super stores, due to they feel to need more time to make purchase decision in order to make the most right choice to buy these any products. They usually expect to stay half hour , even one hour or more time in super stores. Their time pressures are depended on whether what kinds of products that they expect to buy in the super store. For example, if the super store visitor expects to buy one laptop computer. He will expect to make purchase choice decision within half hour, even more time. Otherwise, if the super store visitor expects to buy stationery, e.g. pen and rubber and pencil, he will expect to make purchase choice decision within 10 minutes. So, when the super store visitor expects to buy the product is more expensive, then his time pressure time will be longer than the super store visior expects to buy the product is cheap, such as stationery and laptop two kinds of products.

However , due to super store 's expensive and cheap product consumers whose time pressures are different. So, brands choice number will have much different between them. For laptop example, due to superstore visitors can accept to spend longer time to make laptop purchase choice. So, one shelf can place 5 to 10 different brands of laptops , another shelf can place 5 to 10 different brands of laptops to let them to choose. Otherwise, for stationery example, due to superstore visitors can not accept to spend longer time to make stationery purchase choice. so, one shelf can place less than 5 brands of pens, the another shelf can place less than 5 brands of pencils or another shelf can place less than 5 brands of rubbers , another shelf can place less than 5 brands of rulers to let them to make purchase choice in short time.

Secondly, for restaurant eaters example, when one restaurant has many eaters choose to enter this restaurant to eat its food, then it only chooses to let some eaters to enquire ticket number to queue to wait. Of course, some eaters will not like to wait too long time, so they will leave the queue to choose another restaurant to replace it in possible. For example, in afternoon eating time, these are two busy eaters, the student feels hurry to go to school or the working person feels hurry to go to office after lunch, although the restaurant service staff had given him one ticket to let them to queue to wait. However, their expected queue waiting time is within 15 maximum, but there are many eaters are queuing and their ticket numbers are small numbers. So, they feel that they must not enter this restaurant within 15 minutes themselves limited queue time. Consequently, their late entering this restaurant after 15 minutes issue will influence that they will choose another restaurant in possible. So, the restaurant long time queue will cause some eaters choose another restaurant in busy time. I recommend that the restaurant can limit every eater's eatting time, e.g. it calculate every eater's restaurant entering time and it limits every must leave the restaurant within half hour in busy eatting time. It can post notice to let them to know in the front door, e.g. Every eater needs to leave our restaurant within half hour, otherwise, you will need to bring your food to leave please. So, every eater know that they need to eat all food within half hour, otherwise, they need to bring their food to leave this restaurant. Then, this restaurant can increase more seats to let many queue waiting eaters , they do not queue to spend long time to wait to enter this restaurant. Consequently, many queue waiting eaters will choose to enter this restaurant, due to their queue waiting times are not exceed their time pressure limited time.

The final case is cinema queue . In general, any cinemas will have many audiences need to wait to buy tickets to watch movies. However, if the cinema has many audiences , they need to spend one hour, or two hours , even more than two hours to queue to wait to buy the ticket to watch any movies in the cinema. If some audiences' expected queue waiting times are within one hour. So, if these audiences‘ expected queue waiting timesa are more than one hour. Then, they will choose to leave this cinema and choose other cinemas to replace it in possible. How to avoid these time pressure audiences losing number increases in cinema busy time? I recommend that this cinema ought increase ticket purchase counter service staffs number , e.g. opening more three to five ticket purchase counters number in order to let these one hour time queue time waiting audiences can purchase ticket to watch their movies within one hour. So, opening urgent ticket purcahse service counters number issue is depended on whether there are how many audiences are waiting to buy ticket in the cinema in the time. However, it is only one best way to avoid the cinema audiences number loses in cinema busy time.

● Time press how influences video playing game consumer purchase behavior

I shall explain that why it has relationship between the video game student consumer individual learning time and the working people individual working time both can influence video game playing consumer individual video game choice behavior. I shall assume that the different kinds of video game content difficult or easy win competition and entertainment spending on playing time factor will have more influence how the student or working person individual choice of what kind of video game purchase. Otherwisem evey video game price and brand and video game entertainment design content will have less inflience to every video game consumer individual purchase choice.

Why do the every video game's learning playing time and the playing time is spent to satisfy the feeling of winning game both factors will be the main factors to influence the feeling busy learning student or feeling rest working personal target video game playing consumer individual kind of which video game software purchase choice? Why do feeling busy learning students or feeling rest working people will be prefer to choose to buy the kinds of need spending little time to learn to play to achieve the easy winning of the video game content aim in short time?

Nowadays, the different brands of video game products have different prices, various entertainment design contents and the easy or difficult win content feeling to be promoted to sell to satisfy the students or working people video game players' entertainment needs. However, time pressure will be one important factor to influence students of working peoples' video games choices. I shall explain that the time pressure factor how will influence the feeling busy learning or feeling rest working video game players or video game content software consumers to choose to buy the kinds of video games softwares which can let them to feel to spend little playing and learning time and they can feel easy to win the the video game competition in short time preference in this electronic enterainment video game industry.

Nowadays, video game target customers, they are young students and adult working people in common. When , the student does not need to go to school and he/she stays at home, he /she will like to play video game after he/she finishs to learn just a moment usually or the adult working person finishs jobs on the day, after he/she ate dinner, he/she will also like to play video game at home. So , video game can be one kind of entertainment product to let they feel enjoy to play when they re staying at homes.

Video game can be one kind of entetainment culture or entertainment behavior at home to them in popular. A player's ability to perform within a game entertainment is important, and players tend to knowledgeable about their achievements and failures within any game world. So, when one student hopes toget pass grade in school examination. He will choose to spend little time to attempt to win the video game content competition in short time because it can let him to feel that may increase his confidence to pass the grade in the school examination later in possible when he ensures that he had won the video game content competition. He believes that he can be trained to raise whose judgement and mind and analysis abilitiy in his playing visdo game proceed. Instead of playing video game can increase student learning confidence, it can also increase the working people's confidence, when the working person hopes to be promoted or increased salary later from his supervisor's appreciation. He will attempt to spend little time to win the kind of video game content competition in short time. He will have more condifent to achieve to raise his working performance to let his supervisor appreciation if he can learn how to win the kind of video game competition in short time.

It seems that whether the player needs to spend how much time to learn how to win any kind of video content game competitin , this " spending learning time of winning any video content game competition in time pressure playing environment feeling factor will influence the student or working person 's video game content purchase choice. If the video game design is more complex or difficult to let the player to feel to learn to win the game competition as well as it also needs them to spend more long time to learn to play and win the kind of video content game competition. Then, it has possible to influence the hard learning students or hard working people video game consumers, they do not choose to buy any kinds of need spending long learning and playing time to win the kinds of video content game competitive software products. So, it seems that the spend how much playing and learning time to win the video game content competition factor will bring time pressure to let the hard working people or hard learning student video game consumers choose to buy the video content game software products are easy to learn to play in preference because they expect to pass grade or appreciate easy, if they feel that they can learn how to win the video game content competition in short time as well as they do not spend much playing time to win the kind of video game content competition and they will reduce their learning time at homes.

I shall explain why price won't be the main factor to influence video game players' purchase choices in preference. Some video game software sellers feel reduced sale price can attract many video game buyers' choice in preference. It is one wrong mind, due to video game software price is not too much high, it is one kind popular cheap entertainment software product. So , the kinds of similar entertainment content design video game products , their sale price difference between the kind of most expensive , the highest price video game software and the kind of the cheapest , the lowest price video game software won't be difference very much. Their price difference level may be US 410 to US$50 or even less than US$50 level. So,, one video fame entertainment player won't feel that the kind of similar content design of video game software's higher price which will influence he chooses to buy another cheaper similar of kind video game content design software product to replace to the prior higher price one. Because their price difference are not too much or video game software entertainment product is not on kind of expensive product to let them to feel. So, it seems what video game software price won't influence the video game players' prior one of preference choice, it is not easy to be replaced from later cheaper one, when the video game player feels like to play the kind of high price of video game content software before.

Can the video game content influence player individual purchase motivation in preference? In fact, there are many different kinds of video game contents to let players to choose. This free-to -play busines model that has rapidly speed to achieve games services to general . So, some students or working people players can free download some kinds of video game softwares to play from online channel. It will be attractive to the no paid video game players. Hence, free download video game content will influence the paid video game players' purchase decisions for in -game content are not only affected by people's existing general attitudes, consumption values, and movitations , but also by the design decisions and the needs built into the game by the developers. Because the paid video game players won't like to buy the similar content video games, which can be free download to play from online or internet channel. They will feel infair or not worth or loss if they choose to pay to buy the similar video game content entertainment software, after they discovered that they may be free download this kind of similar video game content to play from internet.

It will bring this question: Why will time pressure influence video game player chooses to download free video game to play in preference? When one student feels that he has no enough time to study, he won't choose to fo to any video game shops to do video game software comparative behavior to compare which one's price is lower, game playing content is more attractive, brand is familar in order to make final purchase decision in preference. If he discovered that there has one kind of video game content, which can be free download to play from internet or online channel . So, when the student feels that he needs have much time to study on the day. Hw will choose to attempt to find some kind of video game contents from computer tool which has the attractive entertainment content , it can let he to feel enjoy to play and it is free download from mobile or computer. Then, he won't choose to spend unpredictive time to visit any video game shops to make purchase decision on that day. So, time pressure will be one factor to influence some video game software consumers to feel whether they ought either visit any video game shops to make purchase choice or download some free video game contents at homes for the feeling no enought learning time student players. Even time pressure will also influence adult working people video game players, when the working person feels tries after his full day busy working on that day. Then, he will want to stay at home to rest . Although, he expects to visit any video game shops to choose which video game software product(s) to buy on that day, but when he discovered taht there are some video game contents which ar attractive to influence him to do free download behavior from internet at home. Also, he feels very tried and he will choose to stay at home on that day. If he can find some free video game contents are attractve to influence he chooses to do free download video game contents behavior and replace visiting video game stores behavior on that day. So, free download video game content entertainment activity will be one attractive promotin video game software method to assist the video game sellers' new video game products to let many feeling time pressure learning or working video game players to know from internet channel.

Consequently, online free entertainment video game content download playing choice will influence many video game shops will lose many feeling time pressure video game players number every day in possible. Also, it means that the lazy students or disliking learning students or no job people or (less working hours) part time working people, they will be the main target video game customers, due to they accept to spend much time to visit their video game shops to choose any kinds of video game softwares to buy in preference.

● How can video game advertisement method influence feeling time pressure and feeling without time pressure video game software consumer purchase purchase?

In fact, video game sellers can choose new media chnnel to advestise their new video game software products, e.g. computer online advertisemen channel, instead of video game pictures in shops, magazine, newspapers, television, radio ,cinema, public transportation tools poster traditional advertisement channels. However, computer online advertisement channel can attract many feeling learning time pressure of students consumers and feeling lack of enough rest time working people consumers to let them to choose to view their video game software advertisements from online websites at homes conveniently.

It is easy to understand , due to these feeling lack of enough learning time student video game players and feeling lack enough rest time working people video game players, they go back home after they finished learning in schools or they finished jobs in workplaces on that video game purchase planning day. After they eat their dinners, they may turn on computers to search information from internet. Suddenly, they discover some attractive video game contents photos or images are advertised from the video game seller's website or public yahoo websie , even they can choose to buy any one of these video game softwares from online shopping channel. Then, they will feel convenient to buy any one of these video game softwares from internet channel. SO, online video game advertisement will be the feeling time pressure video game players' first time contact channel at homes or the fastest advertisement contact channel to compare visiting video game store post advertisement, television , radio , magazine contact advertisement channels, when they are staying at homes.

Due to internet is popular to be used to search any information for consumers. So, the traditional magazine, newspapers, television, radio and visiting video game stores advertisement channels won't be more attractive to the feeling time pressure video game consumers . They will chooce to find any information from internet at homes in preference , when they have at least one computer to use at home, they can click website to search any information from internet easily.

The most important factor is that they can feel to spend little time to search information from internet to compare spending more time to find anywhere places whether they has magazines or book stores to sell video game magazine and newspapers publishers, radios and television won't inform them when they have video game advertisements to let they know whether what new video game softwares will promote to sell as soon as possible when they buy newspapers or turn on radios or televisions at home.

Otherwise, internet will be easy to let the feeling presure video game software consumers to know when whose liking new video content game software(s) will be promoted to sell from internet advertisement easily. Also, the feeling time presure video software consumers can choose to buy their liking video game software (s) from online shopping channel in possible if the video game seller can provide one website to let him/her to pay visa to buy and then it can deliver the video game software(s) to his/her home immediately or tomorrow or later time when the buyer's home located in overseas or far away from the video game seller's warehouse and their softwares are needed to be delivered by air plane transportation.

So, the feeling time pressure video game players won't need to leave their homes to spend more time to visit any video game stores to make final video game purchase decision any time. Hence, online advertisement and shopping channel will be one good sale promotion method to any feeling time pressure video game players nowadays. It will influence the traditional visiting video game stores' video game consumers' purchase behaviors to change to online purchase behaviors at homes conveniently, because they avoid to waste much time to visit video game stores as well as avoid to waste much time to choose any video game products in different video game stores, when they are staying in different video game stores. Visiting video game purchase behavior will need they spend whole day time to make final purchase choice, even it is possible that they can not make any video game softwares purchase decision after they visit many video game stores on that day.

Otherwise , online game advertisment channel can let them to feel to spend little time to search any new video game contents from every web page as well as every web page can show the new video game content images or photos or pictures to let every online users to see clearly when he/she sits down to turn on computer to search any kinds of video game content information to view at home in short time.

In conclusion, online video game advertisement and online shopping channel can attract many feeling time pressure video game players' consideration when they need to search any kinds of new or old video game contents information and it also changes their purchase decision to online shopping from traditonal visiting video game store shopping behavior. Video game industry's advertisement method , sale method is the kind of video game playing content's easy or difficult feeling degree , spending how much playing time to win the competiton in the game entertainment environment factors will influence the feeling time pressure video game players' final purchase decision making choice behavior to any video game software publishers nowadays.

- Time pressure consumption or production situation explanation

Will one consumer feel difficult to make consumption choice or one employee feel pressure to work when the worker works in the company's high pressure productive environment or the consumer makes difficult purchase choice in high pressure consumption environment? Will time pressure bring motivation to the consumer purchase decision or the employee working efficiency? It depends on some factors to either cause time pressure working environment or raise the employee individual efficiency , or time pressure consumption environment can either encourage the consumer purchase decision or discourage the consumer purchase decision . I shall explain as below:

What does efficiency mean? Due to economic problem is a scarcity of resource, efficiency is concerns with the optimal production, consumption environment. For time pressure consumption situation example, e.g.

supermarket shopping counter check out purchase queue waiting time pressure, cinema purchase ticket queue waiting time pressure, restaurant queue waiting booking table time pressure etc. different consumption pressure time waiting situation. For time pressure woring situation example, e.g. supervisor's demand tasks finishing on time before the employee leaves the office on the day, then the supervisor's demand will cause the employee feels time pressure to do all tasks on time, otherwise, he needs to work overtime, even no extra allowance compensation to his extra time loss, or the employee needs to do another employee's tasks , due to he is absent on the day. However, this situation can be called economically efficient production or consumption if: no one can be worse off, no additional output can be obtained, without increasing the amount of inputs, production proceeds at the lowest possible per unit cost. For these economic efficient consumption situation example, the consumer has much time to wait, the shop has less different styles of products to let them to spend time to choose in the shop's shelf.

However, these definitions of efficiency are not exactly equivalent, but all they are caused by the idea that a system is efficient if nothing more than be achieved given the resources available. On time pressure working environment influence aspect, Time pressure working environment may bring efficiency, but time pressure working environment may also bring inefficiency, e.g. employing workers who are not necessary for the productive process. For example, a firm may be more concerned about the political implications of making people redundant than getting rid of surplus workers, or lack of management control, if a firm does not have supervision of workers, then productivity may tall as workers talk it easy, not finding cheapest suppliers, a firm may continue to source raw materials from a high cost supplier rather than look for cheaper raw materials to be supplied to let workers to work in one short time task finishing environment. Then, they may feel short time task finishing pressure to bring inefficiency production result.

I shall indicate efficient production and efficient consumption situations as below:

For building a new airport working time pressure situation example, how to evaluate that it is one efficient productive situation. When a new airport may lead a greater increase in social benefit than social cost. It seems that an efficient productive situation in time pressure workin environment. The time pressure can excite or encourage workers hard to work and the won't feel pressure to work to cause inefficient performance. Therefore, these is a net gain to society. However,those people living near the new building airport will lost out. Therefore, this is not an improvement. However , if the people living nearby were compensated for extra noise, when the workers need to use equipment build the new airport in the pressure building time when they feel lack of enough equipment supplies or lack of enough workers to cooperate to work. Then, it is possible to have a negative improvement inefficient production. So, how to evaluate whether the new airport builders feel time pressure to finish this new airport building project before the due date or not. It can depend on whether the people living near the new airport often listen noise or not. In a without time pressure working situation, the workers do not need often to cause noise in their airport production process. If they feel no time pressure to finish this new airport building gproject before the finishing due date. Their working behaviors ought not often cause noise to influence themselve nervous or emotion to be poor to work, or feeling workload to bring the inefficient performance consequence to finish this new airport after the due date in possible. It ought seem that they won't feel time pressure and they have confidence to finish to build this new airport before the due date. If the employer has enough workers number and equipment supplies number to let them to do this new airport building task. Otherwise, if they need to often cause noise. It implies that it has no enough workers number and equipment number to let them to build this new airport before the due date. They feel time pressure to finish this new airport building project. So , the employer ought increase workers and equipment to reduce their worry about on building this new airport project before or one due date finishing, if the employer hoped that they can perform efficiently.

For avoiding feeling time pressure on consumption situation example, when the product can be allocated efficiency, then consumers will feel less time pressure consumption psychological influence. This occurs when products and services are distributed according to consumer choice preferences. It means that the seller can make more accurate preferable choice prediction whether consumers will choose to buy what kinds of styles of products or characteristics of services provision in preference. So, they won't need to spend more time to do choices to decide whether which styles of products or characteristics of service provisions whom hope to buy or consume in preference.

In one allocative efficient occurs when the price of the product or service is

same to the marginal cost. A more precise definition of allocation efficiency is at an output level where the price equals the marginal cost of production . This is because the price that consumers are willing to pay is equalient to the marginal utility that they get. Therefore, the optimal distribution is achieved when the marginal utility of products equals the marginal cost. For example , when firms in perfect competition are said to product at an allocatively efficient level, monopolies can increase price above the marginal cost of production and are allocatively inefficient. So, if the product is sold in the monopolies markeet environment. Many the similar product sellers raise sale price to sell similar styles of products to let consumers to choose to make purchase decision. Then, will influence them to feel their choices to the kinds of similar styles of products in the time pressure product choice consumption situaton. Otherwise, firms are in the perfect competitive consumption environment. Consumers can feel their similar product prices are not difference too much. Then, they will feel less time pressure to make which kinds of product choice of purchase decision in preference. They will spend less time to make final purchase decision. So, whether the kind of product market is monopolies or perfect competiton which will influence consumers feel more or less time pressure consumption generally. Consequently, consumer time pressure feeling and the kind of product 's market environment, they have close relationship to influence consumer purchase decision making behavior.
What is dynamic efficient production environment? This refers to efficient over time. Dynamic efficiency involves the introduction of new technology and working methods to reduce costs over time,e.g. letting workers feel that productive time can be reduce to produce the same level of tasks. Then, they can avoid long time pressure to influence their working performance. With this mind, we can define dynamic efficiency as an aspect of economic efficiency that measures the speed or the rate at which the production possibility curve moves from one static equilibrium point to another within a given period. For Ford Motor company efficient production predictive method case example, in the 1920 year, the Ford Motor factor were very efficient for that particular year. However, compared to later decades, we can not say that the producton methods of the 1920 year were efficient. On other words, it is important for firms to make best use of given resources. But, they also need to develop greater use of resources over time. Hence, Ford Motor can let workers to avoid time pressure feeling to produce its any motor vehicles i their productive process in 1920 year. When its new

productive technology is adopted to be used to manufacture any kindsof its more vehicles in factory. Also, it can raise their productive efficiency to manufacture any motoe vehicles in 1920 year. However, although Ford Motor can make best use of given resources to assist workers to produce any kinds of motor vehicles efficiently. The vehicle buyers' driving needs or new design motor demands are increasing. They need new different kinds of Ford Motor design to be provided to let them to choose. So, Ford Motor also needs to develop greater use of more resources over time, due to the more different styles of new design motor vehicles are needed. So, the new kinds of productive resources are needed to be develop in order to adopt to vehicle buyers' needs. If Ford Motor can not find or discover any new productive material and it can not innovate any new kinds of productive methods to be taught to let workers to learn how to manufacture the future new designs of Ford Motor vehicles efficiently. Then, they wil be possible to feel time pressure to work, due to they can not adopt how to manufacture the future new design motor vehicles, when they are not proficient to apply the future new productive technology to manufacture any new design of motor vehicles.

This is one good example to explain high technological manufacturing resources and techniques and method can let workers to reduce time pressure to manufacture in their manufacturing process, but if the manufacturer can not improve its manufacturing technology to let its workers can continue adapt how to apply the new different manufacturing method to manufacture the future new design or innovative products. Then, they will be possible that they feel time manufacturing pressure and raising inefficient manufacturing performance, due to the manufacturing technology or productive technique can not be improved and training to them to raise skillful proficiency. So, these productive workers will onle reduce time pressure to manufacture in short time, if the manufacturer can not improve any new kinds of manufacturing techniques and teach them how to apply the future new manufacturing techniques to work efficiently. .Then, their performance will be ppor in possible when they feel long time pressure o work in the long time pressure working environment. Hence, it has relationship between new technique improvement and long or short time working pressure and performance.

Distributive efficiency can raise consumption desire and it can reduce consumer individual choice time to make purchase decision in short time. Concerned wirh allocating products and services provision according to who needs them most . Therefore, requires an equitable distribution . Distributive efficiency occurs when products sale ans service provision are consumed by those who need them most. Distributive efficiency is concerned with an equitable distribution of resources because of the law of diminishing marginal returns .

The law of diminishing marginal returns states that as consumption of product increase the product users tend to get diminishing marginal utility. For example, if a family already has three cars, but gets a fourth car, this fourth car will only increase this family net utility by a small amount. If by constrast someone on a low income is able to get their first car, the marginal utility will be much higher. Therefore, to be distributively efficient, society will need to ensure an equitable distribution of resources. For car sale case example, if the car seller has distribution of resource, such as different styles of car kinds sale number efficiently, e.g. the high quality expensive car number manufacturing number is less than the low quality cheap car number. Then, there are many low income people may have enough time too pay to buy the cheap car in the car sale market. Then, it is possible that the car company can seel more cheap cars in short time, due to many low income people do not need to spend long time to consider whether they ought buy or not buy any first car, even another car or other cars for their family to drive. They will not feel purchase time pressure to make final car purchase choice, due to there are many common low quality cheap cars number are supplied to be sold in the country's car market immediately. So, when the car company can concentrate on manufacturing many low quality cheap cars to prepare to sell. Although, its high quality expensive car number reduces, and it will increase its high profit earn in possible in short time only. Otherwise, in long time benefit aspect, many low quality cheap cars sale number will increase many low income car buyers nu,bers when they find the car manufacturer can have many different style design of low quality cheap cars to let them to choose more than other car competitors in the country's car sale market.

In long time, it will reduce time purchase choice pressure to its car consumers, when many car buyers believe this car company only it has many different styles of design low quality and cheap price cars to let them to choose to buy to compare other brands of car companies in whose country. Then, they won't feel need to spend extra much time to choose other brands of cars to compare this car company's cars. It implies that the country car buyers only consider to spend less time to choose this brand of any cars to make car purchase decision in preference. They won't feel time pressure to consider other brands of any kinds of style cars purchase choices often habitually.

So, this brand cars have built choice habit to many low quality and cheap car buyers in this country. So, when the seller can build long time brand of any this car company's any car products choice habit to let many buyers this brand cars are preferable choice, then they will prefer to spend short time to make purchase decision for this company's any cars . Then it can sell any low quality and cheap cars to compare other brands of car companies more easily.

Reducing time pressure to traveller behavior

● Time Factor Influences Traveller
Behavior

How working time influences airport employee performance ? Why does the employee choose to do whose behavior to perform in the working environment? What are the general factors to cause his behavioral performance to bring his job performance effect in the working environment? In simple, I shall indicate some factors to explain how and why they can influence employee individual chooses to perform his behavior in any working environment in generally, These factors will influence how the employee perform his behavior and why he performs his behavior when he feels his behavior or peformance is more satisfactory to his organizational demand or need. Then, I shall indicate some different organizational cases to attempt to explain why and how these factors cause the employee performs his behavior in his organization as below chapters.

Firstly, I shall indicate different time pressure factors can influence why and how the airport employees decide to do his performance in any organizations in generally as below:

(1) Organizational causing factor

What does one organization mean? An organization means human creations, rather than buildings, equipment,machinery etc. It can include industrial, commercial , educational, medical , social clubs, etc. different kinds of organizations. In general, staffs within any organizations will feel need to work to achieve the organizational goals, and co-ordinate their activities for any missions. Each department's staff individual behavior or performance have relationship to be influenced by structures, informal or unofficial groups and structures can be at least as important as the formal organization structure. So, it seems that any different organizational structures will influence their staffs' behavior or performance indirectly or directly. Each employee will have one unique or idenified role in the organization. " The roles people play rather than the personalities in the roles" (Perrow, 1970, p.2). So, each staff will feel or he will know what will be his role playing and the interrelationships between organizational structure and role playing factors , they can cause how each staff decides or chooses how any why he ought need to do his behavior in order to adapt his organization's working environment need or demand.

In general, in bureaucratic model of organizations, where work is organized and conducted on an entirely rational basis, such as government's any departments, which are usually bureaucratic model of organizations. The essential features of a bureaucracy are: Specialization of division of labour , a hierarchy of authority, written rules and regulations, writting memos or notices for any tasks message, reports are more needed more than oral message to be communication channels within the organization's different departments' coordination. Hence, in bureaucratic , staff individual will consider to do any tasks or perform whose behavior carefully in order to avoid error occurrence, or is encountered complains by clients or same level staffs or his supervisor or manager within himseld department. So, organizational structure factor will influence how and why its employee decides to do behavior or performance when he feels his behavior is more rational or suitable to adapt him organization's need or demand.

(2) Staff individual work psychological factor

Miller (1966) explains psychology means what the science of mental life. Mental life refers to three phenomena: behaviors, thoughts and emotions. However, in any organizations, employees will have any characteristics of work psychology to influence whose performance or behavior in any working environment. For example, when the employee feels stressed, he will feel thoughts and emotion to be negative or poor as well as he also feels fear the he can not finish his tasks to let his supervisor or manager feels unhappy or he will complain his working performance is inefficient , even he will dismiss him on the day or later. Then, his fear emotion will influence he may not cooperate with his other same level of staffs in their team easily. It is one good feeling stresses at work case explains how and why the employee will perform worse or poor level suddenly in any organizations. For another example, when a group of staffs need to make decisions, and the extent to which, a person's attitudes towards particular groups of staffs can influence his or her behavior towards them within the department. The organization's team leaders, e.g. manager, supervisor, CEO, he/she will need have good emotion managing ability and managing ability to perpare how to manage his/her teams to cooperate work together in any teams efficiently. In this high stress working environment, the high stress feeling employee will need to judge how to do his behavior in order to manage his teams work together efficiently daily. Hence, some attention is also paid to defining how situations differ from each other psychologically. The high level leader or CEO position managing staff will need to know the supervisor or manager's personality and psychological characteristics tendency how to influence their behavior, think and feel in certain ways in order to let he/she has more confidence to manage the different departments' managers or supervisors more easily , such as the CEO, the top level leader. So, the top level, CEO needs have good work psychological knowledge to know how to manage his/her middle level, such as mangers , supervisors more easily. Then, he /she may have more confidence to manage whose organization efficiently and effectively. So, when the top level employee , such as CEO can know every middle and low level manager or supervisor individual personality characteristics factor. Then, he/she can increase more confidence to know how to manage each department, each team in low and middle level organization structure more efficiently and effectively. So, the working psychological factor will influence how and why the top, middle and low level employees how any why decide their choice to do their performance or behavior in consequently. For example, it is usually that when the employee feels how job satisfaction, then he will choose to perform worse working behavior because he feels that his manager does not consider what kinds of tasks are his interesting jobs. So, his dissatisfaction will influence his working performance to be poor or worse to compare his prior working performance when he feels more bored or low dissatisfaction to himself tasks. Then, his dissatisfactory job feeling will influence his emotion to be worse or poor as well as he will perform more worse or behaves more worse in order to let his manager or supervisor to feel. It is possible that he wants to use worse working performance or worse working attitude to let his manager or supervisor to know his job dissatisfactory or bored feeling. Then, he can encourage his manager or supervisor to change other new and interesting tasks to let him to attempt to replace current bored tasks in possible.

(3) The social and economic factor

Iles and Robertson (1989) have recently pointed out that there has been relatively little work in personal selection which has looked at the issues involved from the perspective of candidates. The only candidate-centred area of work which features extensively in the personnel selection research literature concerns the extent to which selection procedures are fair to different sub-groups usually ethic minorities or women of the population. A large amount of research material focusing on this issue has seen produced. A variety of terms such as bias, adverse, impact, fairness and differential validity are used in the literature or this issue and a clear grasp of the meanings and definitions of some of these terms of some of these terms is crucial to an understanding of the research results.

Hence, when one staff feels that his manager or supervisor is often treated to let he feels unfair or biases simply to compare the other members of different sub-groups in whose team. Then, his unfair treatment feeling how and why to choose or decide to perform whose working behavior to be worse to compare his prior working performance or behavior So, the unfair feeling treatment factor will influence the employee chooses to perform poor or worse working behavior or working performance, because general employee usually feels that it is one important channel to let his supervisor or manager to know his any job-related unfair feeling emotion is caused by the impact of unfair personnel selection procedures factor influence.

Normally, of cours, the extent to which a fair selectin method is related to job performance, it means that when the employee feels that manager or supervisor can let him to compete to do this job in fair selection method as well as he can earn more reasonable or fair salary to compensate whose job ability . Then, he will attempt to perform better in order to satisfy his manger or supervisor's job demand. Otherwise, if he feels that he can not earn the higher salary level, due to that he needs to do the lower level job -related task unfairly, but in fact, he believes that he have ability to do another better position and earn more salary in this organization. Then, he will perform worse to complain whose organizational unfair selection treatment to him.

So, the reasonable and fair personnel selection procedures on candidates factor will influence the organization's any staff individual performance. In consequently, all of these factors will influence how any why some staffs perform worse or better. Then, I shall inficate some cases to let readers to attempt to judge whether which of above these factors can cause these organizations‘ employees to choose or decide to perform their behaviors in their organizations in order to adapt their working environment easily. You can learn to judge whether time pressure is the main factor to cause your organization's employee individual performance to be worse or any other main factors accurately.

Reference

Iles, P. A. and Robertson, I.T. (1989) . The impact of personnel selection procedures on candidates. In Herriot, P. (Ed.), Assessment and selection in organizations. Chichester: John Wiley.

Miller, G.A. (1966) . Psychology: The science of mental life. Harmondsworth: Penguin.

Perrow, C. (1970). Organizational Analysis. Belmont, Calif: Wadsworth.

- Airport time consumption factor

Instead of airport is one arrical and leaving terminal station place main function for any travelling passengers after the airplances had landed on the country airport's subway. I feel that airport has also another main functions. It can help the country to attract more travellers to choose to go to the country to travel as well as it can persuade them to raise consumption desire in their whole journeys after they leave the travelling country's airport if they feel the country airport's service performance can satisfy their short time staying need. I shall explain why any countries' airports can influence travellers‘ travelling destinations and travelling shopping choices to be increased or decreased.

The future airport will be the assistance role to assist tourim industry development. The factors include, for example, safety and terrorism control, when the travellers feel the country's airport is safe to stay when they catch air planes to arrive the coutry first time. Then, the country's airport can build safe image to let them to feel the country is safe to travel indirectly, traditional cirport service providers will need to seek new service way to deliver value, such as subscription based service models can let travellers to feel the country's airport can provide one comfortable and enjoyable short term travelling staying environment in the country's

airport. Then, they bring pleasant emotion to prepare their journey trip after they leave the airport in the foreign country.
So, if the country's airport can let the travellers feel safe and comfortable , then it can bring new exciting and enjoyable feeling to the country's image. Because airport will be any travellers' first time arrival place after they catch airplanes to arrive another country. So, positive or negative airport's image will influence travellers how they feel whether the country , it is worth to choose to travel indirectly. However, airports need have good facilities to satisfy any related airplane service employees or any airport food or product businesses need, instead of travellers' need. For example, it needs have good allocation of terminals and access to facilities , they will be managed and regularly reviewed and regarded their good facility availability , capacity constraints and the best use of available facilities to satisfy any food or product sale shops' sale need and airport passengers' purchase need both in airports or airplane pilots, airplace service employees, irport security employees' comfortable working environment need.
However, airport inside and outside also needs to be arranged enough parking space facilities to let any aircraft parked or stored at the airport from the place where it is parked or stored in order to let any vehicles to be parked in airports or ouside airports easily and conveniently. When any sudden emergency matters occurred, the aircraft subjects to unforeseen operational delays , it should need to contact airport operations control centre to indicate when the expected time of arrival and departure is, there is no need to request a new slot in cases of unforeseen operational delays where the operation will take place within 24 hours of the agreed slot time. For example, of unforeseen operational delays include aircraft technical issues or weather conditions that could not have been planned for. Hence, operationally delayed aircraft must utilise slots in the same manner as originally agreed. If any change to the original slot agreement is required, e.g. a slot must be requested immediately. Moreover, when aircraft subjects to non-operational delays must request new slots immediately, following the correct process in those conditions of use, an example, of a non-operational delay may include delay caused by late running passengers or poor schedule planning. Hence, airport needs have good facilities and communication system to coordinate to any departments to avoid aircraft unforeseen delays to cause airport passengers feel nervous and brings negative and poor emotion to the airport's service performance.
On airport baggage handling function aspect, airport operators must comply

with the baggage policy made available to all operators with the airline business management team. For example, where a flight destination or carrier is identified as being at significant or high risk, the operator will pay a charge as notified by management, equating to the cost of any policing cost additional to the services normally provided at the airport for carriers or destinations at lower levels of risk. In fact, airport baggage management needs be checked and delivered in order to help any airplanes' passengers to transport their baggages to follow their airplanes to be delivered to their same destinations when their airplanes are flying with the passengers and whom baggages to arrive the same country's airport at the same time absolutely. So, barrage management operators need submit or demand and in agreed format the already fleets absolutely, such as fleet detail to report these data to include aircraft type and registration, number of seats maximum take off weight kilogrammes of each aircraft owned or operated by the operator, in order to avoid any passengers' luggages wrong delivery occurrence in possible.

Hence, any airports must need to consider above basic passenger service operation in order to avoid any accident occurrences to bring poor airport service attitude feeling. If airport management expected that they have good service performance to satisfy travellers' short term staying needs in themselve countries' airport.

- Airport time management strategies

Any countries' airports expect to increase passenger movements, they must have effective strategies to carry on reviewing any errors and improve performance effectively. For instance, how to keep cost effective measures to lower operating costs and keep good performance on quality, such as for maintenance and cleaning airport cost reducing measures to introduce variable, performance -based elements to encourage productivity gains, how to manage and implement new technological systems to improve information flow and work processes within the country's airport, e.g. airport e-immigration system can allows to receive real-time alerts on any airport building faults. It can reduce airport reliance on manpower in these areas, thus reaulting in better productivity and cost savings for long term airport expenditure. So, high technological strategy system is needed to implement to any country's airport in order to facilitate the handling of more aircraft movements to optimise aircraft handling on runways. Their benefits include reduction of departure flights separation times, reconfiguration of flight routes, and improvements in runway inspection processes.

These new measures can bring effective in improving any country's airport's runway efficiency, developing new infrastructure including the extension of the taxiway, roadway and power supply networks. It aims to satisfy travellers' convenient transportation needs when they arrive any countries' airports and prepare to find suitable transportaton tools to arrive their destinations more easily (airport transportation roadway, taxiway building network strategy).

Hence, any countries' airports need have good strategy to manage a wide range of activities and risks, which are broadly classified into strategic , financial operational, regulatory and investment. Any countries' airports also need to seek how to reduce the occurrence of risks and to minimum potential adverse impact as much as possible, uch as airport risk management strategy. Because when the country has many people are living and they need often to catch airplanes to leave their countries to travel as well as there are many foreign travellers choose to travel the country. Then, the country's airport must need to expand size and raise good facilities, e.g. more automated immigration gantries are needed to be installed, taxi waiting areas are also needed to be explanded with additional taxi bays constructed to accommodate the higher number of arriving passengers , even increasing airplane subways number to satisfy many airplanes need to fly away from the country's airport or coming airplances fly to the country's airport's landing on runway needs often.

So, airplane subways number expanding strategy and cutomated immigration gate fast checking system is needed when the country has many travellers choose to go to the country travel and/or many local people need to leave themselves countries to travel. For instance, departure and arrival immigration control as well as pre-boarding security screening will be controlled for more efficient deployment of manpower and equipment. Moreover, in the line will the trend of self-service options of airports arrived the world, provisions will be made to have more kioslls for self check in,self-bag -tagging and self bad-drops. The increasing use of these options will help airlines and ground handling agents reduce processing times and staffing requirement. For example, a fully automated to reduce reliance on scare manpower baggage check in and check out system, the baggage handling system will also be equipped with ergonomic lifting aids to enable heavy and odd-sized bags to be handled with ease, even by older workers.

Then, the country's airport must need to increase subways number and immigration fast checking service facility to avoid handling passengers crowd queueing problem often occurs every day. When any airports often let passengers feel time pressure to queue to spend long time to wait immigration checks and leave the airport. It will bring their negative emotion feeling to the country's airport. Then, it is possible to influence they choose to go to the country to repeat travel again. Hence, the country's different airport strategies are needed when the country has increasing travellers number trend as soon as possible.

Another strategy concerns airport emergency service on safe aspect. Any countries' airports need have a highly trained specialist wait that is positioned to provid fast action rescue and fire protection for passengers' life safety ,e .g. aircraft rescue and fire fighting vehicles are needed airport. An incident command and control simulator which provides realistic and interactive simulations of emergency scenarios for the purpose of any sudden accident occurrences in any countries' airports.

So, any countries' airports need to develop an internal digital system to ease labour-intensive work processes like fire safety inspection, incident reporting, logistic management and recording of its personal fitness results, with the new safe system , data entry is needed mobile enabled with the use tablet computers. For example, the airport safe unit can continue to enhance its emergency preparedness and rescue capabilities with the successful staging of two drills, simulated aircraft crashes on land and at sea, as well as any exercises validated crisis contingency plans are recommended to earn strong capability in coordinating rescue efforts involving both the airport community and mutual aid agencies in order to carry on rescuing passengers and airport pilots and service attendants whom life safe service when air planes are crashed on land and at sea.

Another strategy is now aviation facilities strategy, it can support fly, cruise and fly-coach initatives, important options to a rising number of interm travellers, if it can be implemented successfully. It can bring enhancement measures benefits, includes the reduction of departure flight separation times, reconfiguring of flight routes and implementation of aircraft speed control for increased runway use efficiency.

Hence, one successful airport operation , the airport management needs to know how to implement the traveller check out or check in service functions when they arrive the airport or leave the airport and to satisfy its passengers' short term terminal station staying or transfering another airplane's flying need as well as it also needs to know how to implement its different strategies to improve its service performance and to let passengers have more confidence to the country's airport service operators' behavior and they also feel safe when they are staying the country's airport. Hence, any travellers' short term staying feeling in the country's airport , whether the country's airport can bring either positive or negative emotion , which will influence they choose to go to the country to travel again in possible. Hence, airport management can not neglect how to improve airport service performance to satisfy any first time or more time airport visitors' short term staying need.

- Long time airport staying and passenger consumption relationship

It is an interesting question: Can the country's airport service performance influence passengers consumption desire? Nowadays, travelling is a kind of popular entertainment whn working people have holidays, retired people have more savings and students need to go to holiday to feel rest time after they had hard to study. They will choose go to other countries to travel. So, " freguent travelling times" which will increase to any travelling consumers. If the traveller often chooses to go to the country to travel, he must need to permit to enter the country from its airport immigration. If his every visiting time to the country's airport, he feels the country's airports' staffs services are poor performance and he feels that they are not polite or rude attitude to treat him when he needs to check out or check in from the country's airport immigraton gates, even he feels difficult to enquire any airport service staffs, either he feels difficult to find them or they need to spend long time to let him to queue to wait enquiry, even he also needs to spend long time to queue to wait check in or check out in airport immigration gates when he arrives the country's airport or he leaves the country's airport.

All of these negative airport staffs' service attitudes and poor service behavioral feeling, they will cause the frequent traveller doubts whether the country is a worthy travelling place and it is possible to led his negative consumption desire in the country's airport. Then, all of these negative emotion will influence the frequent traveller reduces consumption in the country's airport , even wothut any consumption in the country's airport, when he visits the country to travel every time. So , it seems that airport's service performance will influence travellers carry on more or less

consumption in the country's airport. Then, it will influence all the country's airport related retail and restaurant businesses' sales to be reduced indirectly in the country's airport.
Instead of airport service performance intangible factor aspect, the airport's clean, airport itself appearance attractive design, large size and shops and restaurants' suitable locations and internal environment design etc. these tangible factors will also influence travellers' consumption desires in the country's airport. For example, in one special day, e.g. Olympic Games day, the Olympic Games country's airport may complete in record time and its airport can successfully handle a estimate record 85,000 minimum departing passengers a day during the Olympic Games period, twice the number on normal days. Travellers and media will describe the Olympic Games country's airport retail shops and restaurants consumption experience as seamless, magical and unforgettale airport staying experience, if the Olympic games country's airport can provide an excellent service performance on the Olympic games period. Then, it will influence the increasing sale amount in the Olympic Games country airport retail stores and restaurants during period. So , when the country is experiencing special day, such as "Olympic Games " is chosen to carry on competition in the country. Then, in this Olympic Games period, it will attract many travellers to choose to go to this country to travel, due to they have interest to watch Olympic Games competition in this country. This country's airport will represent this country's image. If it 's airport service staffs can provide excellent service to let any one of travellers to feel when they are staying in this country's airport short time and this country's airport itself appearance and design can also be changed more attractive and beautiful and the airport's retail stores and restaurants also design more attractive and beautiful. Then, the travellers' consumption desires will be possible to raise , when they visit this country's airport in first time in this Olympic Games travelling period.

● Global air transport network time management

In the future, if the country has a strong and affordable global air transport network, it will bring more advantages. Due to many travellers expect to catch air planes which can fly to another country in short time , it can reduce accidents occurrence chance on sky or on sea. So, short time flying can be more attract to compare long time flying. So, it explains that why many travellers prefer to choose one way flying more than transfering another /other air plane(s) flying. Although, they need to pay more air ticket fee. So, if the country's airport can have more subways number and large subways areas to let many arrival air planes and leaving air planes need to fly from land or fly to land in the country's airport frequently. Then, the travellers can buy any air tickets to book same day or next day or later day flught time to fly to any country to travel more easily, when the country's airport has large area size and many subways to let many airplanes can stay in its aircraft subways in same time. Then, the country's airport flight frequency will increase , it means that there are many travellers can catch airplances to fly to other countries in any time very easily from themseleves country's airport. It is time-sensitive feeling to let the country's travellers, they can feel to fly to other countries to travel in short day. They do not need delay to fly to any countries, when the flight airline is either full seat or the time can not permit any air places land on the country's subways.

So, none delaying time sensitive travelling frequent flught model will be one attractive flight flying method to influence the country's travellers choose to frequent travelling behavior. Because they do not change their travelling day, due to airplanes have no enough seats supply or the country's airport has no enough land subways to let any airplanes to stay to cause delaying their flight travelling booking seat day expectly.

So, airport is similar to airline to need to use different customer relationship management to attract returning travelling customers . It brings this question: What are the most attractive motivation factors in airport travel market?

I believe that factors may include airport loyalty, various flight time arrangement distribution channel, passenger check in or check out, laggage safe delivery, airpor security service. Moreover, flight schedules are also a main factor influences the travellers' final travelling country choice decision among different travelling countries. However, if the country's airport can build good loyalty image when passengers are staying in the country's airport in short time, it can show a more attractive motivator to increase travellers' consumption desires when they are staying in the country's airport in short time.

Hence, airport 's loyalty seems have relationship to influence travellers' consumption behavior when they are staying in the country's airport. For example, when the different countries' travellers feel enjoyable and happy to stay in the country's airport longer time. Then, their airport long time staying behavior will raise their consumption desire and chance to find any right restaurant to eat food or drink or find any right retail shop to buy right products in airport. Hence , when the country's airport can buil loyal customers relationship. Then, it will bring the advantages or benefits to the airport's any retail shops or restaurants on sale growth aspect, such as : their retention rates will go up easier, their customer referrals will go up easier, the country airport retail shopd and restaurants travelling customers whom spending rates will go up easier, the country airport retail shops and restaurants customers will be loss price sensitive, the costs of retail and restaurant servicing then will go down easier. Hence, if the country's airport customer service performance can maximize travellers' loyalty. It will influence travellers to feel the country airport's retail shops and restaurants have more loyalty to compare other countries airports' retail shops and restaurants loyalty.

So, it implies that any any country airport's loyalty will have relationship to influence its travellers how they feel the country airport's retail shops and restaurants' loyalty. Due to loyalty is intangible and it is obly feeling. So, when the travellers have positive emotion and wheh they are staying in the country's airport long time. Then, they will have positive emotion to spend more time to walk around in the country's airport as well as when they are passing any airport's retail shops or restaurents. Their pleasant emotion may encourage their consumption behaviors to have interest to find any right restaurant to eat food or drink or find any right retail shop to buy any right product in the country's airport in preference easily. Because they had been accepted to spend long time to stay in the country's airport, when they feel interest and surprise to visit the country airport when they arrive. Moreover , the long airport staying time will increase their purchase chance to any the country's airport's retail stores or restaurants in the country 's airport in first time visiting.

● Long time waiting pressure brings negative expectation to airport passengers

When one country's airport can satisfy passengers expectation to accept its service demand, then profitability and passenger number will be influenced to increase. So, airport management needs to focus on how to satisfy any passenger individual need or expectation when he/she needs to stay in whose country's airport for wait to either transferinf another airplance need to carrying on check in or check out in the country's airport immigration gate need in short time.

However, because if the country's airport service can let its passengers feel happy , then they will be super spenders to spend airport staying longer time to consume or entertain in the country's airport. Moreover, it will bring any the country airport's retail shops or restaurante to earn more sale growth indirectly. So, any country airports need to consider how to bring excellent customer services for any passenger individual need in airport. Because its service behavior or performance will have indirect relationship to impact the county airport's any businesses and itself any parking , entertaining services income in airport.

" The concept of managing airport customer expectation on passenger service quality" will be any country airport's main aim. Basically, airport passengers‘ perception concern how the airport service staffs' service attitudes or performances influence how they feel either negative emotion, such as anger, dissatisfaction, irritation, neutrality or positive emotion, such as happy, satisfaction, pleasure, delight. So, when the airport passenger individual perception is better , then his expected to the country airport individual service staff level will be at the highest level, but if his service expectation is less than his expectation standard, then the airport passenger will dissatisfy with the lowest satisfaction level to be influenced the country airport's other any one service staff by the one airport service staff whose poor performance. Because any one of the country airport's service staff , every one will influence the country airport's image. Of every one has excellent service performance, then, it will let many different counties‘ passengers feel sympathetic emotion from their every one's behavior. Otherwise, if every one has or most service staffs have poor or not considerate ot not sympathetic service attitude to be let them to feel, then any one of them will let many itself airport's countries' passengers feel the country airport's image is poor. They won't like to spend long time to stay in the country airport, even their short time airport staying behaviors will influence the country airport's any retail shops or restaurants businesses sale growth to be reduced from their short staying time influence.

In general, airport service staffs need to spend some time to answer any passengers‘ enquiries. So, how they answer their enquiries will influence how their achievement in order to raise the country airport's passengers satisfactions. It may lead a rise in different countries'passengers‘ loyalty and retention, therefore the country airport can increase many different countries passengers number when the repeating airport visitors , they prefer to choose to go to the country to travel again , due to its airport is attractive reason in possible.

So, any country airport management ought have a policy from how the airport established desirable standard performance, measure it against actual performance to action taken once and revise any unachieved acceptable service level to the acceptable excellent passenger service performance in the country airport. For example, any country airport needs to manage and identify the target passenger segmenation target groups and to make bettwe understand the key elements that have the greatest impact on meeting every different target passenger segmentation group individual expectations and needs from their services in themselves country airport. So, any country airport will have relationship to any one of airline, as well as any one airline will have direct relationship to every passenger when he/ she stays in the country airport in short time.

However, instead of restaurants and retail shops; sale relationship will be influenced by the country airport's service performance, airport management also bring more empahsis on non-aeronautical (non related airlined and retail business) revenues, such as shops rents, concessions, car parking service income, consultancy and property developed diversified service incomes. So, airports need to focus directly to enterainment travelling airlines' passengers, meeters, and greeters, business-travelling passengers , users of general aviation services and transfer air plane short time staying visitors, or lone time staying visitors, e.g. the passengers need to live airport hotel for on night or more than one night sleeping before they catch the airplane on the day. So, all these different target passenger segmentations will have different service needs in any country airports.

However, airport passengers' behaviors and expectations of the airport experience depend highly on the types of traveller, they include: demographic characteristics, (i.e. gender, age group, income, sex, occupation) , purpose of trip (i.e. leisure, business), and their circumstances. In general , the passenger can be divided into different group, such as arriving, departing and transfer with different expectation and need, in the way they will be using the airport services and facilities different need and will also influence the behavior of individuals when in the commercial area. For example, passengers who are departing and arriving will require all airport facilities including: car rental, rail, buses access, pre-booking taxi service, check in or check out service, bad processing and security check and vertical and horizontal moving in passenger terminals. Otherwise, transfer passengers will have a short waiting time in airport and their needs will be likely different from those of origin and destination passengers. Some of the transit passengers will need to spend one hour, even more than four hours or half day in the airport. By providing airport facilities that can accommodate their needs, such as a place to lie down and take a short sleep time, free shower, free email public service will mostly give than an enjoyable airport experience. Evem some handicapped people or old people who feel difficult to walk in the airport corridor. Then , the airport will need to arrange the auto -wheel chairs and auto airport vehicle facilities to let service staffs to provide electronic auto wheel chairs to let them to sit down or drive the auto airport vehicle to sit down with them to go to their destination in the airport's any places immediately. For passengers travelling with families may want children play areas, where kids can have a great time when waiting to board the aircraft. They also want the availability of rooms of families travelling with badies equipped with changing facilities, baby crib, microwaved and hot water need. When passengers are on business trip, may want a lounge, with all the business, facilities that they can feel free to use, such as free internet access and other services , such as fax, scan and photocopy machine. Hence, any airport managements need to develop the strategic customer facilities providing service in order to improve the design and delivery of all the facilities and services need by understanding expectation of each passenger segmentation group in their airport staying time.

Finally , in airport unique design aspect, our global airports will need have different unique design to let any travellers to feel that the country's airport can have its unique design to let themm to feel the country airport has itself own airport culture or entertainment features to attract they observe its appearance in order to achieve the increase more travelling visitors number when they feel enjoy to stay in the country airport longer time before they leave the airport. I shall indicate different countries' airports how they will perform themselves different airport cultures and unique design as below:

For China and Hong Kong Chinese airport design example, their airports need have Chinese cultural feeling to let Western travellers to feel their airports' designs and cultures are different to any Western countries' other cultures. So, China anf Hong Kong airports' designs can increase many old big size building photos number in their airports to let foreign visitors can walk on the long glass walkway corridor , when they enter walkway coddidor to walk through different 100 more airplane leaving and arriving gates number and the ground floor is built from heavy glass material. So , any one foreign traveller need to walk through on the long glass walkway corridor to pass any one gates to arrive his/her airplane leaving and arriving gate location and catch airplance to fly. Also, the glass walkway ground floor can let them to see the airport's vehicles and airplanes and people and trees outside environment clearly when they are walking on the airports' all glass material manual made ground floor. It will let foreign travellers feel China and Hong Kong airports building designs are different to the foreign countries' themselves airports' designs as well as Hong Kong and China airports' old building photos will let all leaving passengers feel difficult to forget their old building historical photos and they will know hoe their architectural skills are developed to imprved to build nowadays unqiue desing method from traditional building design method in Hong Kong and China airports. Otherwise, for US, Uk etc. foreign countries their airports designs can increase underground floor fish pool architectural design outside to their airports in order to let any passengers feel that they can see many different kinds of various fishes are swimming. So, their outside large fish pool can let them to feel surprise when they are staying in their any airports, e.g. one beautiful large size fish pool, it can be built to close to their airports and the fish pool can have various kinds of big and small fishes swim in the pool to let passsngers to see, or their airports can appear suddenly and unexpected of a gaping hole in the airport's outside ground, known as a sinkhole. Sometimes, the airport's outside sinkhole will fill up with fresh water to become deep , shaped manual made sinkhole to let passengers to feel they need to enter to the sinkhole and then they can enter the airport. So, the outside large size sinkhole will attract many passengers to stat to observe how the fresh water is entering to the sinkhole interestingly. Then, they will feel surprise when they need to pass though the sinkhole , then they can enter the airport.

In conclusion, attractive airport architectural design will let any passengers can not forget that they had ever visit the country to travel in their travelling experience as well as they can be influenced to like to stay longer time in the country airport by the airport's attractive design and environment influence. The most important influnece, it can influence airport related business income when they like to stay longer time in the airport.

CHAPTER THREE

Hospital organization effective time management strategy

1. What do you understand by the concept of a time management model to hospital front line service staffs Critically discuss their relevance to a public sector service ,such as the hospital.

A effective time management model reflects the fact that companies can generate revenue through a variety of combination of the basic price and prices charged for optional additional items. Some price models may be sustainable by giving away a product at very low price initially, but then charge higher prices for essential items that are needed to make the product function. Sometimes, the dominant pricing model in a market is challenged by a new entrant, with the result that consumers' expectations are changed. The price model can occur in perfectly competitive market or non perfectly competitive market.

A perfectly competitive market characteristics include there are many producers supplying the market, each with similar cost structures and each producing an identical product. No single supplier on its own influence the market price because it is not monopoly, water and electricity is managed by government to control the public utility company which can not charge high fee to every householder user at the reasonable price ; both buyers and sellers are free to enter or leave the market and there are no barriers to entry or exit and there is a ready of information for buyers and sellers, for example about competing alternatives, e.g. oil products and stock markets where shares are bought and sold are exist in perfectly competitive market. In perfectly competitive markets, firms are price taker and their ability to set prices is limited by the level of demand and supply within the market they serve. If the total demand go up, all other things being equal, the going rate of prices in the market for their product will rise. Likewise, if there is a drop in total supply for whatever reason (e.g. because of bad weather, there will be further pressure for prices in the market to rise. The final price paid in the market will reflect the balance between supply side and demand side factors. When the organization has effective time management to have enough goods supply to be kept in warehouse to let consumers to buy any kinds of products or foods. So, the product price will have more reasonable to let consumers to feel because when the warehouse has enough goods and it means that none any goods shortage to raise price to sell to them. The model of perfect competition presented the forces of competition may be ideal for consumers because the tendency of market forces to minimize prices and/or maximize firms' outputs. But in such markets, suppliers are forced to be price takers rather than price makers. in a perfectly competitive market, firms are unable to use marketing strategies to affect the price at which they sell. At a higher price, buyers will immediately substitute identical products from other suppliers. Lower prices would be unsustainable in an industry where all firms had similar cost structures.

● UK hospital lacks effective time management challenge case

Otherwise, an non perfectly competitive market, firms are able to use marketing strategies to affect the price at which they sell. I shall dicate one UK hopital how to apply effective time management strategy to raise front line service staffs confidence to service their patients and patients' families and friends and car park needers to let them to feel satisactory to their services. Such as UK medical service market , private hospitals and public hospitals and clinics which can raise their service fee to their patients to follow their patients demand due to their doctors and nurses service performance, medicines quality and price and patient beds supplies factors to influence their service charges to their patients in UK. Hence, NHS needs to provide different and excellent medical service to its patients to make them to feel it's service is better to other private hospitals and clinics if it wanted to apply price model to its car parking or hospital phone system service charge to its patients because it is a public sector medical service organization. It ought not charge extra service fee to its patients in its hospitals. If it charged extra service fee, such as car parking and hospital phone system service which are same or higher or lower than other private hospitals or clinic , which need to ensure which medicine quality, doctors and nurses performance which are better than private hospitals and clinics and its patient beds need have enough supply to any patients when who feel need to sleep in its hospital. Because NHS image is a non profit medical organization to any UK poor patients, who choose NHS medical service are due to its medical service charge is cheaper than private hospitals and clinics and who feel it can provide free car parking and free hospital phone system service.

A market is defined here need not be a physical location where exchange takes place (as happens in retail and wholesale grocery markets). A market in the economist's sense refers to all individuals and firms who wish either to buy or sell a specific product. A market is defined in terms of products or service and geographic description, so the UK soft drinks market refers to all individuals in the UK who seek to buy soft drinks and the suppliers to that market. The UK medical service market structure can describe as the number of consumers, such as patients and medical providers , such as private hospitals and public hospital , such as NHS (National health service) and clinics; the barriers that exist to prevent new private hospitals or clinics or public assistance hospitals from entering the UK medical service market (or prevent UK patients do not prefer to choose NHS medical service); the extent to which the supply medical services is concentrated in the UK small number patients normally and the degree of collusion that occurs between patients and/or private or public hospitals or clinics medical service providers in the UK medical market. Governments often seek to regulate the prices of key products and service, such as electricity and telephones and public hospitals medical services, so it is important to understand how firms can reconcile the sometimes conflicting approaches of market forces and regulation, such as NHS public sector medical service in United Kingdom. Of course, if NHS public sector medical service planned to charge some non major service fees, such as car parking and hospital phone calling service to its patients and hospital visitors and staffs which are same to private hospitals, it needs to consider pricing model should never be seen as an isolated element of hospital's marketing decision making. It needed to consider its service performance of its doctors and nurses, its social responsibility of public medical service image whether it is better or worse than private hospitals that it had created and NHS 's distribution strategy whether it's patient beds supply numbers are enough to patients and whether it's medicine quality and supplies and prices which are reasonable to compare to private hospitals or clinics in this medical service market in United Kingdom. Private business organization with a broad range if products or services are often price different with their portfolio in quite different ways. So, lacking effective time management will cause hospital's service fee raises because hospital feels there are not enough nurses and doctors and counter front line service staffs to serve their patients. So, effective time management will avoid to increase nurses and doctors and front line service staffs number and salary expenditure and reduce their pressure when they need to serve many patients and their families and friends when they need to spend long time to queue to wait their any kinds of medical service arrangement.

- How to implement effective time mangement to hospital

They may have developed a time mangement control to avoid hospital service fee increasing , due to not enough nurses and front line patient room front line staffs service to patients ot their families or friends when they need to spend long time to queue in hosptial. So, time management is important to influence them feel less pressure to work in hospital, which describes the way that it uses pricing of its portfolio to maximize its overall revenue. Hence, one product or service may be charged at a very low price, on the assumption that it can raise higher price if many clients choose to buy its product or consume its service. In some sectors, a number of different pricing models co-exist. For example, in the emerging multi-channel television broadcasting market, some channels are provided free of charge to users, but make revenue from selling advertising space, when others charge to users, either on a monthly/annual basis or a pay to view basis. The idea of a pricing model is familiar to private sector organizations, but do they have a role to play in the public sector? In the UK, pricing models are increasingly being discussed and developed for services which have previously been considered a vital service and available freely to all.

Adrian, P.(2012) showed that the National Health Service (NHS) has a long and proud tradition of providing health service to all, according to an individual's need, paid for out of general taxation, according to individuals' means. Pricing has historically had very little role to play in the NHS. However, from the mid-1990 year, individual NHS trusts began exploiting charges for ancillary services as a means of boosting their revenue. One of the first targets for charging was users of hospitals' car parks. Trusts argued that providing car parks was not central to the mission of NHS trusts, and conveniently, government was encouraging more people to use public transport and leave their cars at home. Critics argued that patients were essentially captive and public transport was not a realistic alternative for most people. However, it showed that at one hospital in London, a patient who attended A&E on the advice of her GP, was charged UK$3.75 for the first two hours' use of the hospital car park and UK$7.5 thereafter. She was ten minutes over the two hour period and therefore had to pay higher charge. She also questioned the fact that charges were reduced to UK$1 per hour after 6:00 PM, when many hospital departments were closed. For private sector service, a lower evening price, when there is not much demand from customers, and plenty of spare capacity, it quite common. But is it right that a hospital should only charges lower prices at the not busy time when much of the hospital itself is closed? If lower prices are designed to stimulate additional demand, it this a realistic prospect when many hospital departments are only available between 9:00 AM to 5:00 PM? Another source of revenue exploited by many hospital trusts from the use of bedside telephones by patients. Many trusts entered agreements with private telephone service providers which allowed incoming and outgoing patient calls only through the officially appointed system, which used a premium rate number.

A proportion of the revenue was retained by the hospital. Conveniently, hospital trusts pointed to evidence that mobile phones could harm sensitive medical equipment , and therefore used this to eliminate competitive pressure from patients' mobile phones, forcing them to use the hospital's own telephone system. The ethic of hospital telephone pricing was challenged by the House of Commons Health Select Committee, which accused some trusts of using excessively outgoing call, adding to patients' costs, and boosting hospital revenue. It cited a hospital in Essex where people wishing to telephone patients were being charges 49p per minute at peak time and 39p off peak. By comparison , a typical household rate for a long distance phone call was around 7p in the peak and 2p in the off peak. The select committee also expressed doubts about whether a ban on mobile phones in hospitals was actually a result of possible interference with medical equipment and recommend visitors should be able to use mobile phone within certain areas of hospitals. So, it seems that UK private hospitals patients phone calling service fee is below than householder phone calling service fee and it is not every patient must need to use phone when who stays in hospital as well as the visitors should able to use mobile phones and who should not use hospital phones within certain areas of hospital, who will not interference with medial equipment. Otherwise, by banning mobile phones, had private hospitals been more concerned about creating a monopoly environment for pricing their telephone service, than any possible risk to their equipment? However, I think National health service (NHS) which is one public government assistant hospital, it can not be same to private hospital to charge unreasonable car parking fee or hospital phone service fee to its patients, due to these ancillary services is not hospital main income source and it is one non profit hospital, it needs to provide the fair and non expensive medial charges to its poor patient segment because who are not rich, so who will prefer to choose NHS medical service to compare to choose private hospital services in United Kingdom.

National health service (NHS) is a privatization, fragmentation and market competition of health care provision supposedly to cut costs and improve the efficiency of the health service in England. The NHS was set up in 1948 year to be a free and accessible care, publicly owned and funded sector service in England. NHS needs to consider to redefine its relationship with health service, limiting the quality and quantity of care it can expect to receive, how it access that care, who is delivering if and even how it is paid for. The result will be poorer, fragmented services with larger differences in quality and access. Services/treatments will cost more and the public will increasingly have to pay for aspects of its care that used to be free at the time of treatment. Traditionally privatization has been through the sale of public assets and services to private owners through the mass sale of shares, e.g. the sale of telecoms, railways, energy or water services. These companies than own the services and are able to make profits from them like any other are able private businesses. In the NHS until now, this model of privatization is taking place through a combination of the reduction of the role of government in regulating health provision, the transfer of services to the private sector through commissioning from any qualified providers, such as independent sector treatment care centers, outsourcing of parts of services to the private sector, the creation of market mechanisms for the distribution of funding within the NHS (e.g. commissioning, payment by results mechanisms, the purchaser-provider split and so called patient choice policies). The use of private finance initiatives that use private money to build new buildings and infrastructure and then the state has to pay, the creation of foundation trusts that are run much more like private businesses and have the ability to raise funding through private patients that pay for services, allowing services to become not for profit organizations, such as social enterprises, cooperatives or mutual and thus leave public ownership, limiting access to certain services previously provided by the NHS. Provided healthcare tends to cost more. It requires a large bureaucracy to operate, with huge transaction costs that come with contracts, billing and litigation. In general, as the proportion of private spending on health care rises, so does the overall cost.

The creation of healthcare market can also impact upon the continuity of care people receive. There is always the threat that the private sectors or other providers who take on a service that doesn't secure the expected financial returns may cut losses and withdraw from the provision of that service. NHS is under increasing financial pressure. For example, surgery like hip and knee replacements are more expensive areas of care, the results cause the loss of training opportunities for junior doctors expenditure spending and other health professionals as ever large shares of routine surgery and medical procedures are diverted away from the NHS. Centers for research and medical innovations are also threatened. This can lead to service being out. NHS hospitals will therefore fail financially and be pushed into greater debt. This could lead to hospital mergers, closure or the private sector coming in to run the service on profit making contracts. NHS will bring poor health care service if it will not increase its service charge price to patients. The poor service will be caused, such as permanent damage may have been inflicted on patients with serious conditions due to the lack of follow up care after treatments. In a second worrying example dangerous delays affected the patients of a privatized out of hours. A competitive market system leads to greater rationing and gradually drives patients to take on more responsibility for funding their own care. It seems this already in the privatization of long term care and dentistry. Patients may soon have to top up the cost of their hospital care in the same way that many already do for community health services. The concern is that the NHS will provide a less comprehensive range of treatments. For the private sector, the aim is to make a profit from every contracts, which is not the same as providing the best service . For example, Southern Cross, where the need to make profit lead to the rapid closure of care homes, leaving old people with no home. Hospital people with learning disabilities and challenging behavior were subject to physical and psychological abuse. Privatization will lead to fragmentation of the health services. This is a process on a commercial footing and redesigning the system along market lives. With different organizations delivering different service in different locations, it is also likely to lead a new health service with some area receiving much better care than others, hardest, leading to greater health inequalities. Fragmentation of services leads to worse clinical outcomes as staff have less opportunity to work in a fully integrated dynamic multi disciplinary team. Patients with complex needs can be particularly considerable.

The impact of privatization on current NHS staff, who are transferred from NHS employment to non NHS organizations would be changed terms and conditions at the time of transfer. These terms and conditions could be changes at some time in the future, staff would no longer be covered by the national negotiating arrangement in the NHS, meaning they would not be entitled to any future pay uplifts or agreed charges to the change terms and conditions of service . If staff moved from this employer to another outsourced community service, who would lose their entitlement to access the NHS pension scheme and would be treated as new staff rather then former NHS staff, the new service provider could argue that the service who will be providing is so different that they will not be requiring staff to transfer. Those staff will than be made redundant. In conclusion, NHS is one public medical service non profit organization. It's pricing model ought be public service price model, such as no price discrimination and non competitor based pricing aim. It may be difficult or undesirable to implement a straightforward price-value relationship with individual of public services for a number of reasons: Such as NHS public sector medical service pricing can be actively used as a means of social policy, subsidized prices are often used to favor particular patient segment groups, such as car parking fee charges to visitors or hospital staffs only as well as hospital phone system service charges to visitors only or prescription medical service charges favor the very ill and unemployed patients and low income patients and students patients.

2. What factors should influence the level of car park fee raises.

I believe that effective car park time management can let many visitors can find any vacancy to park their cars and avoid car park service fee increases to let them to feel unsatisfactory when they can not find any vacancy to park their cars in the hospital in possible. Also, it can bring busy time car park parking fee increases , if the hospital often has any

vacancies to let them to park their cars in the hospital car park in possible. Principles for fair hospital car parking, such as NHS is important because its car park service represents the hospital reputation. Charging for car parking is often necessary, but needs to be fair, providing a travel plan for users of all types of transport, controlling parking fairly, with concession for those whose health conditions or work commitments mean they have to park frequently or at anti social hours, showing car park and transport costs and how charges are invested, thinking about the environment and how transport can reduce the NHS 's impact , being open and involve patients and the public. It is important to get car parking and transport policy and it is
communication, right to ensure fair access, good patient and staff experience and to protect hospital organization , such as NHS reputation. Clinical and social changes as car ownership to patients, staff and visitors to hospital sites has increased. For services with rural or urban , as public transport infrastructure is less convenient and reliable . When for specialist treatment, some patients need to travel greater distance and modern hospitals have often been located on the edge of population centres.

Car parking is also a factor in patient's experience of using healthcare. When much progress has been achieves to improve the patient environment inside the hospital, including cleanliness and new buildings, patients frequently report dissatisfaction with transport and parking arrangement. Visitors concerns both cost of car parking and also the availability of space for people with an essential need, illustrating the competing demands that managers need to balance. Patient experience is an important objective for hospitals; poor experiences can undermine confidence in clinical quality and stress can be worsened by poor transport and parking policies. Car parking can have a major impact on the local and national reputation of the NHS hospital . As patient choice increases, reputation and loyalty will be key drivers for provider's commercial sustainability. It seems car parking is one important factor to influence patients who choose hospital more than location/ transport/ easy to get to/ reputation of consultants factors. Ensuring that patients can access hospital when they need to is an important part of healthcare delivery. Many patients who need to travel to hospital by car, either because of mobility or illness, a lock of alternatives or through choice. However, providing a car park is not the only component of a travel plan. Access to healthcare should be considered in terms of service planning, decisions on location of services, building design, access routes and the other transport modes. One of the factor of the current changes to the way that NHS hospital services are delivered is that healthcare should be localized where possible. In many cases, people who used to have to travel to hospital are being treated in community health centers. The NHS hospital can also ensure services are accessible. Most notably, ease of access has recently been improved by reducing waiting times and by enabling patients to choose and book their appointment at a time and location that is convenient to them. Another of factor is whether NHS hospital had or had not ran a bus service from a nearby park and ride car park that runs every 15 minutes. The service has proved popular and is now run by the UK country council.

The hospital is been to extend the shuttle service to the other three park and ride car parks which serve the city. The other factor influences NHS hospital charge includes the control parking fairly with concessions for those whose health conditions or work commitments mean they have to park frequently or at anti-social ours. In order to ensure that those patients who really need to access hospital by car are able to NHS often need to ensure that car parking space is available on site. Space is usually constrained, NHS hospital is in city or town center with high land costs and planning constraints. Charging some patients, visitors and staff to park can manage demand for space when ensuring that those who really need to park are able to access services. Where charging is required to manage demand, the overriding principle should be to ensure that where possible those patients who have the greatest need to park are prioritized. Where managing demand is a reason for charging for car parking, there may be scope for varying rates for different times of the day and the week, for example, increasing charges for non essential users in peak hours but applying a minimal charge at night when there is less reason to ration space. As well as prioritizing car access for those with greatest needs restrictions on car parking may also be required to deter non hospital traffic, particularly where NHS hospital is located in controlled parking zones, near shopping centers or other facilities that might need to illegitimate required use of NHS hospital grounds. In these cases , NHS hospital may be required to be charge the same as local car parks to avoid abuse by non visitors. However, alternative arrangement could also be explored, including day permits for people with appointment. NHS car parking fair policies should need to be fair application. This is often a cause of concern for patients and visitors.

Concessionary schemes and season tickets should be well publicized and available, since a patient may not known in advance low frequently who will need to attend a clinic in the next month. Penalty charges, or towing away should only be applied extreme circumstances with a presumption of good faith that no patient or visitor chooses to stay in hospital longer than necessary and may how on arrival how long who will have to wait for treatment. Running a car park can be expensive. These are maintenance, security, insurance and running costs and the NHS hospital has to pay for the space the car park uses. Costs are particularly high where land prices are high or there is increased risk of crime. At the same time, patients and the public rightly don't expect healthcare to suffer to pay for parking. The transport costs of non car owners are not subsidized by the NHS budgets to provide subsidized free car parks . To make car parking fee would be to penalize those using public transport. Therefore, fair charging is often the most sensible answer to adopt these two demands. Climate charge and pollution and congestion factor also have health impacts. Reducing car dependency is also a public health objective in order to reduce traffic accidents and increase physical activity.

These NHS organizations have a number of environmental and health reasons to seek to encourage people to use other modes of transport. Parking charge together with the expansion of alternative bus an cycling options to encourage a modal shift from cars to alternative transport. Patients , visitors and staff need to be made aware of these aims. NHS hospital can achieve a travel plan to develop to its car parking with the aim of during a period of busy time reducing single occupancy car journeys by 15% over three years, ensuring tat patients and visitors do not have to search for a space for more than ten minutes at peak times, encouraging the number of direct bus routes to the site to increase reducing staff parking spaces per employee by 10% as staff numbers grow. Car parking charges were introduced as part of the plan with certain categories of staff on exempted from charges (night and weekend staff, disabled staff, volunteers, car sharers and tenants of residential accommodation. From an environmental perspective, NHS travel plan supposed to reduce numbers of cars arriving at the site and the numbers of bus car raise. It aims to improve bus services to cause air pollution at the busy car parking period and cycle parking spaces and improved cycle facilities have encouraged staff to commute by bike. Additionally, a park and ride scheme aims to reduce car traffic of the NHS hospital in the busy time.

Moreover, it is absolutely wrong to charge cancer patients regardless of income, for unavoidable parking costs. From a staff point of view, NHS hospital car parking is an indirect tax on healthcare. However, most unions also support the aim of reducing car usage, as long as policies are fair. Because NHS hospital needs to develop transport policies for patients requiring regular cancer treatment. This approach has potentially negative publicity into a positive image to public. These ought be free parking for the duration of a cancer patient treatment or as often as is needed. So, effective car park time management can avoid raising car park price will be needed to let this hospital visitors feel unsatisfactory and angry.

Service-line time management strategies for medical organizations

● Time Management Strategies to Provide Patients With Superior Customer Service

Any hospitals or medical health service organizations , if they can consider patients are they asset or capital principle. Then, I believe that their patients number won't be influenced to reduce by poor health service performance in possible. Due to medical is one kind of service industry, so learning patients psychology how to let they feel health service performance satisfaction is one important factors to influence any kinds of medical service organizations in success, such as dentist, doctor, facial, hospital, etoc. different medical organizations.I believe that these patient service performance factors will influence their patients number to be increased or decreased as below:

1. Start seeing patients as customers. Taking care of patients is what healthcare is all about. It may be hard for some people to think of patients as customers, but they definitely are. Their choices bring thousands and even millions of dollars into a hospital's coffers. In most cases, they don't necessarily need to use your hospital, even though you have Dr. Brightstar on staff. They may end up at the institution down the street that treats patients better.

2. Be courteous and respectful. Always, always, make sure patients are treated with courtesy and respect. I know executives who pretended to be patients inside their own institutions and were shocked by the lack of focus and concern they received. Treating patients has become simply a job for many healthcare professionals. They manifest boredom with their jobs by treating patients indifferently. That's not professional and it's bad business!

3. Never show indifference to patients. It can be quite disappointing at some

urban hospitals and even at some suburban settings. If the illness is not life-threatening, patients are virtually given a number and told to sit down and wait. Many otherwise competent and even brilliant healthcare professionals give patients the feeling they are an inconvenience and a bother. Patients should not be made to feel inferior and misinformed.

4. Don't contradict, argue . Telling patients they are wrong about anything is just plain rude. Even when they have incorrect information, they still should be accorded respect. If you disagree with them, politely explain why their point of view isn't necessarily correct. Your goal should be to explain and communicate, and then to continue to explain and communicate. Help patients understand what is going on as treatment is being given. Patients should feel they are just important, in the scheme of things, as you are.

5. Tell patients you appreciate their business. Everybody likes to be thanked when purchasing an item in a retail store, but in all too many healthcare venues, saying "thank you" is seen as inappropriate. You know as well as I do that saying "thank you" has magic vibes for any kind of relationship. Go ahead and try it! It's a great way to receive your customers' repeat business.

6. Use plain terms and simple explanations. It may be fun to throw around complicated jargon, but it results in misunderstandings and sometimes errors. Nobody wants errors in today's healthcare environment. Always make sure your explanations are not clouded with excessive and complicated verbiage. Be brief and to the point. True professionals go out of their way to explain things in simple, declarative sentences.

7. Good manners are part and parcel of confidence and competence. Don't hide the truth even if it creates problems for you. Treat patients the way you'd want to be treated. Saying the appropriate words can show respect. Establishing eye contact is also part of good manners. Go way out of your way to show respect to others! It's what being civilized is all about, isn't it?

8. Keep seeing healthcare as a calling. Too many professionals begin to see healthcare as a job rather than a calling. There's a big difference between the two. When healthcare becomes a job, mistakes are not far behind. Today there are so many complicated variables in healthcare that it is easy to get off track. Remember who you are and what your core business is. It might help to recall what brought you into the healthcare field. Was it to take care of people or was it to make a lot of money?

9. Stay in touch with patients. Many healthcare professionals don't think they have the time to stay in touch with patients after care is rendered. They tend to think it's unnecessary and creates too much stress. That rationale

should never be tolerated. Staying in touch with patients, even if it's an e-mail or a phone call, will pay off.

10. Keep your promises. Many promises made to patients are never kept. Things like, "You'll get the best care here" and "We treat each individual who comes to us with dignity and respect" and also, "You'll be just fine in a week or so." The difference between empty talk and promises is that promises must be kept. And if it turns out you overpromised, own up to it. Being honest will pay off later. Any quality business must keep its promises.

● Service-line time management strategies for hospitals

For hospitals battered by competition, trying to be all things to all patients is no longer a viable strategy. One way hospitals can more effectively compete with smaller, more focused competitors is to organize themselves by service line, focusing on building world-class capabilities in just a few clinical areas. Hospitals that succeed with this strategy can achieve fiscal benefits while enhancing their ability to serve their communities. But as three disguised case studies show, the successful implementation of a service-line strategy is no mean feat.

Choosing the right service lines to emphasize requires a superior understanding of a hospital's economics and competitive environment. Hospitals also need to overhaul the management of both strategic and nonstrategic service lines. The full-service, general hospital—still the mainstay of acute-care delivery—is under attack. Immense clinical complexity; the advent of performance transparency for evaluating quality, service, and costs; and growing competitive intensity are challenging the notion that any hospital can excel across a broad spectrum of clinical service lines.

Consider a small or large size hospital of average size, with roughly 100 to 200 staffed beds and a mean daily patient census of about 100. On any given day, it might admit only a handful of patients with similar conditions. Contrast this with the current crop of sophisticated, focused, multispecialty institutes for heart, cancer, or neurological care: they treat up to several hundred patients each day. "Pure play" specialty hospitals and outpatient centers with low-cost structures, limited complexity, and focused, high-quality service are also emerging. Competitors like these are raising the performance bar for general acute-care hospitals and, in some cases, posing serious questions about their sustainability.

● Changing traditional medial service to innovative medical service front line service method

While traditional general hospitals are unlikely to disappear anytime soon, a new approach—a commitment to clinical service lines as an organizing paradigm, much as many corporations organize themselves by business unit—is becoming a necessity for many such organizations. Specializing in a few service lines allows hospitals to build a critical mass of patients in select areas and to enjoy economies of skill and scale. In some doctor and nurse past service experience, hospitals that make the leap to a service-line orientation become more productive, improve their quality of care, recruit physicians more effectively, and build market share. By developing a focused service-line strategy, hospitals can also limit their investment in nonpriority areas, with savings to be found in areas ranging from marketing to new technologies. Some hospitals may even choose to take facilities off-line if they are unlikely to reach minimum effective scale in any individual service or combination of service areas.

The transition to service lines is about much more than introducing a new vocabulary or high-level concepts into business planning and strategy. Full implementation of a service-line approach requires real changes in organizational structure, incentive plans, physician relationships, and business development, as well as in many support functions, including IT and human resources. To make wise decisions about which service lines to emphasize, hospitals must have a deep understanding of their own economics and competitive environments. Furthermore, running a hospital with a service-line orientation requires new approaches for recruiting the clinical staff, for aligning its interests with those of the hospital, and for measuring success. Hospitals that succeed—whether or not they are nonprofit institutions—can reap tremendous quality, cost, and service benefits and avoid turning themselves into specialty hospitals, closing their emergency rooms, or lowering the level of care they offer their communities. They will become far more effective competitors as well.

Three portraits few medical service organizations have captured the full potential of a service-line transformation. Issues complicating the transition include : the effort required to reorient a hospital's structures and systems, the leadership commitment needed to shepherd the change process, the difficulty of assembling the high-quality data needed to support good decision making, and the risk aversion of many staff members and physicians. Patience is also necessary—many changes won't yield results for months or even years.

As three disguised case studies show, full-service hospitals face a range of challenges and opportunities when developing a service-line focus. Like many general hospitals, these three organizations have been caught in a vicious cycle of declining resources and patient volumes, as well as a diminished ability to offer high-quality care and to serve those members of their communities most in need. The cycle of decline often begins when transparent information about the quality and pricing of hospitals becomes available—making payers and patients more value conscious and fueling the rise of focused competitors that can attract the most valuable patients. For example, competition is raised for skilled physicians, who see investing and working in specialty and pure-play facilities as an increasingly attractive career option. At a recent gathering of 250 cardiology practice managers, roughly 70 percent reported that their practices had either been purchased by pure-play or specialty hospital groups or had entered into discussions for purchase. Meanwhile, reimbursement rates for Medicare, Medicaid, and commercial patients aren't rising as quickly as a hospital's costs for treating them.

For example, a small size hospital served one million residents across three separate hospital campuses and had a 55 percent share of its city's inpatient cases . Each of the hospitals determined what services it would provide, and the result was duplication and subscale programs. All three facilities offered open-heart surgery programs; as a result of this overlap, each hospital performed fewer than 100 such procedures a year, far from the 300 to 400 needed to keep surgeons and staff clinically competent. Complications and mortality were 40 percent above average. Maintaining three separate subscale programs was also expensive, and the open-heart service line operated at a loss of $1 million a year.

However, when one hospital can attempt to innovate its medical service. Within four years, it may successfully raise its market share to 25 percent, from 20 percent. But it hadn't scrutinized the demographics or payer-reimbursement dynamics—and therefore the profitability—of the new patients it attracted.

Medical equipment must be important to influence patients service feeling, e.g. surgen service. So, any hospital must need to pump money into its loss-generating emergency department, if it was failing to invest in upgraded operating-room and imaging equipment for its highly profitable spinal-surgery unit. This new equipment would have raised productivity significantly and helped to attract and retain valuable physicians. Instead, some hospitals neglect market share in spinal surgery service and they can not spend much money to buy the new medical equipment to serve their patients and in a number of other profitable specialized service lines , they won't increase surgeon patients number, due to they can not own the innovative medical equipment to serve their patients in hospitals.

One hospital was trying to compete across a range of transplant services, including heart, kidney, liver, and bone marrow transplants. Fierce local competition sent the hospital into a downward spiral; it took on unprofitable cases and performed too few procedures to maintain clinical expertise or even the recommended safety standards. When it discovered poor clinical outcomes were the result. Liver transplant surgeons and hepatologists began taking their cases to other hospitals, where heavier case loads and experienced support staff helped ensure a higher quality of care. The less patients hospitals recognized that to improve its clinical quality it had to attract more transplant patients. But its efforts yielded disappointing financial results because the hospital focused on disciplines where revenues were highest, without regard to profit margins.

- Poor time management influence medical cost and charge to patients service fee to be raised

However, to execute a service-line approach, hospitals must first gain a strong understanding of their economics—down to the level of specific clinical activities—and of the growth potential of various service lines. This change of focus involves learning more about the competitive environment, referral patterns, and the possibility of cross-selling other hospital services to current patients.

Understanding current economics Hospitals should aim to understand their profitability by diagnosis-related groups, payers, physicians, and service lines before they undertake a new service-line strategy. Standard billing approaches usually make revenue numbers straightforward, but costs—and hence profit margins—are another thing. For many hospital services, each patient and procedure is different; therefore allocating costs is far more complicated and expensive for them than for manufacturers or retailers. An accurate cost-accounting system is a prerequisite for effective service-line planning. Simply relying on surrogates (such as volume, payer mix, or revenues) can be deceptive and leads, in many cases, to incorrect conclusions.

When the hospital realized that the expansion of its emergency department was shrinking its profit margins, the hospital began analyzing cost-accounting data to determine the profitability of patients and service lines. When a hospital understands where its true profitability lies, it can also negotiate contracts more effectively. When one hospital implemented a service-line strategy, its ought make negotiations with payers involved simply pushing for higher per-diem reimbursements. Armed with the new service-line-specific economics, the hospital greatly improved its strategy for negotiating with the managed-care plan that provided 65 percent of its commercially insured volume. By projecting cost trends on a procedure-by-procedure basis, the hospital learned that for certain cases (where resources used and lengths of stay were more predictable), it would derive greater benefit from per-case reimbursements. It pushed the payer to make the switch, and the new contract soon increased profits by more than $10 million—a 16 percent jump in the annual yield. Estimating growth potential Deciding where and how to focus also requires an understanding of the growth potential for different service lines. An analysis of competitors and referral patterns, as well as a comprehensive clinical understanding of disease pathways (the biological mechanisms that allow diseases to progress), can all uncover growth opportunities.

● Learning similar medical service competitors service attitude and medical service provision method to compare difference

Competitive factors and referral patterns. Understanding the competitive footprint of a service line requires knowing whether community needs are currently being met. Although information about the number of potential local patients and market share is available through public sources , data from these sources often lag by up to two years. To develop more current growth forecasts, hospitals should gather their own demographic data, including the number of underinsured and uninsured patients in an area.

The referral patterns of physicians are another key to estimating a hospital's market potential, since their preferences, together with those of patients and insurance plans, play a major role in a patient's choice of hospital. Moreover, physicians help determine whether cases are referred for treatment, thereby limiting the effective size of the market when cases are indicated but not referred.

For each geographic area that the similar medical service organizations served, the hospital's business-development office mapped referral volumes of key physicians—from primary-care doctors to specialists to doctors affiliated with the hospital—to better understand shifts in market share. Hospital analysts, in contrast to their previous approach, which relied on rarely codified anecdotal evidence, interviewed staff and physicians, much as medical-device and pharmaceutical sales forces commonly do. Learning how rival hospitals influence physician referrals offered insights that helped develop countermeasures to gain market share. Hospital administrators responsible for building relationships with physicians started reaching out to them, and the hospital enhanced its continuing medical-education programs for certain strategic service lines. In addition, a revamping of the Web site, direct-mail system, and advertisements of the hospital raised awareness of it both among referring doctors and prospective patients.

Well-prepared hospitals evaluate the growth potential not just of initial care episodes in a given clinical area but also of related services. To do so, they must understand how patients typically flow within and between service lines. Such an understanding requires hospitals to study disease pathways, likely treatment regimens, and relevant treatment technologies. For example, along with a local physician group, the hospital then invested in a heart failure clinic and began making more regular contact with patients. It turned out that many of congestive heart failure patients could benefit from device therapy (such as implanted defibrillators or ventricular resynchronization). The hospital's focus on its long-term relationship with heart failure patients was critical to its success. Just as retailers and financial-services companies use customer data to their advantage in building enduring relationships, providers increasingly recognize the value of advanced customer-relationship-management techniques. When and where changes are necessary Identifying the most competitive service lines is only half the battle; hospitals also need to change the way they operate these service lines. Rewards for success can be substantial. For example, one hospital have purchased many new medical equipment, if it increased its annual profits by about $15 million within two years of undertaking an ambitious service-line reorientation. I believe that its medical equipment can let many surgeon patients feel medical service satisfaction.

- Poor time management influences front line medical staffs number increases

Changing people processes Implementing a service-line strategy requires changing how a hospital manages human resources. Hospitals may need to recruit more people for critical service lines and fewer for others. Not least important, the professionals and staff of each service line must understand the new strategy and accept the plan so that they will be willing to change the way they work. Incentives that encourage the staff, particularly physicians, to act like owners—including more formal joint-ownership structures, such as equity sharing, investment partnerships, or even full employment—are typically necessary to align the physicians' interests with those of the hospital.

When on hospital changed its personnel processes to support its advanced cardiovascular service line and its elective general-surgery program, which focused on breast cancer. The hospital filled talent gaps by recruiting new physicians (including, for instance, a radiologist with experience and interest in mammography) and increased training to ensure the clinical competency of the operating-room support staff. Before updating an existing joint business plan to improve the alignment between the new goals and the interests of the relevant specialists, the hospital conducted extensive conversations with them. Measuring progress When it comes to performance, most hospitals track only gross patient volumes, net revenue, and, sometimes, hospital-wide profit margins. But to ensure that a service-line strategy is working, they must also track patient-level performance.

For every patient admitted and diagnosed, a hospital might assign a score indicating the clinical outcome and monitor both the cost to treat the patient and the patient's total charges. These cost-accounting figures, plus yields from managed-care contracts, are vital to tracking a hospital's progress. Furthermore, because service-line strategies may take years to implement and show results, it is important to track process milestones (such as the recruitment of key physicians) and traditional measures such as profit margins or the total volume of cases. Like many hospitals, Springfield General found that quarterly performance scorecards helped it track both its financial and nonfinancial performance at a greater level of detail than had previously been possible.

Measuring performance with this degree of precision is challenging, so hospitals should consider taking interim steps. A hospital might use the ratio of costs to charges from each department to gauge a service line's performance. Knowing how every patient is admitted (through the emergency department, electively, or by referral from a specific physician group) can help the hospital to uncover patterns of unusually high or low profitability or possible sources of additional volume.

In addition, tracking how much a hospital actually collects for a service line (after writing off bad debt) can help to judge its true profitability and inform future contract negotiations with payers.An added benefit of detailed performance metrics is that their use often generates a virtuous cycle of improved clinical outcomes. Hospitals should track outcome-specific patient-level data (for example, the time from the arrival of a postsurgery coronary-bypass patient in the intensive-care unit to the point when the patient no longer needs the help of a ventilator to breathe) rather than more generic measures (such as whether discharge instructions were delivered). The more specific approach allows hospitals both to pinpoint areas of care that need improvement and to reward effective performance by the administrative, managerial, and clinical staff.

Managing service lines that aren't a priority In most cases, service lines that are not a strategic priority will continue operating at some level to help hospitals meet basic community needs and cover fixed costs. Hospitals should avoid investing large amounts of capital, their physicians' management time, or executive leadership in nonpriority service lines. But such clinical areas often employ dedicated nursing staff, support personnel, and physicians, most of whom have a vested interest in the status quo. Hospital leaders must develop an effective communication plan to lay out the rationale for change and to set the staff's expectations. The hospital should tell its employees that it will maintain high safety and quality standards but probably won't be an early adopter of expensive technologies in these service lines and won't respond to competitive forces.

For the emergency department, when the hospital choose to limit capital investments, marketing budgets, and efforts to reach previously unaffiliated physicians, as well as to reallocate a portion of the department's expanded space to a gastrointestinal diagnostics unit. The initial reaction of the emergency department's physicians was predictably negative, but by communicating the strategy effectively and sharing the data underlying the decision-making process, the administrative team eventually gained the confidence of the medical professionals, including those in the emergency department. It also used this transparent approach to reassure the broader community that the new strategy was in its best interest as well. Although the emergency department was scaled back, the community benefited from expanded colorectal-cancer-screening outreach programs and gastrointestinal-disease seminars for both the public and the primary-care community. So, emergency department medical equipment need is essential to any hospital service improvement if the hospital hopes to innovate its medical service to let any emergency service patients feel satisfactory.

● What 4 Factors Should Determine a Hospital's Service Line Strategy?
These include the hospital's mission, market growth, margin and the likelihood of the service line's success, as well as the following factors:

- Hospital mission: Type of patient care (secondary, tertiary, quaternary); types of education; and types of research.
- Market growth: Growth by service line; payor mix by service line; ability to feed into other key profitable service lines; and the ability to partner with payors and/or employers and shift share.
- Margin: Payor mix by service line; impact of reimbursement changes; and ability to partner with physicians to control costs.
- Likelihood of success: Necessary investments, such as physician recruitment and capital expenditures; internal capabilities; and competitors' capabilities.

The rate at which these lines are expected to grow is not directly correlated with their profitability, however. For instance, out of those five specialties, orthopedics is generally third in terms of profits and General surgery is the most profitable. Hospitals will need to cross-examine each specialty's expected market growth and its profitability, as service lines across hospitals and geographies can present different clusters of performance. While this data can help hospitals prioritize their service lines, some qualitative factors also need consideration, such as competitors' capabilities. Do competitors offer any specific services within their service line? Do they provide key feeder services for your hospital? Also, what is physicians' perception of competitors? How aggressively do they market their service lines? These questions can help bring a greater understanding to how likely a hospital service line is to succeed.

● Time management learning similar medical service competitors service attitude and medical service provision method

Competitive factors and referral patterns. Understanding the competitive footprint of a service line requires knowing whether community needs are currently being met. Although information about the number of potential local patients and market share is available through public sources , data from these sources often lag by up to two years. To develop more current growth forecasts, hospitals should gather their own demographic data, including the number of underinsured and uninsured patients in an area.

The referral patterns of physicians are another key to estimating a hospital's market potential, since their preferences, together with those of patients and insurance plans, play a major role in a patient's choice of hospital. Moreover, physicians help determine whether cases are referred for treatment, thereby limiting the effective size of the market when cases are indicated but not referred. For each geographic area that the similar medical service organizations served, the hospital's business-development office mapped referral volumes of key physicians—from primary-care doctors to specialists to doctors affiliated with the hospital—to better understand shifts in market share. Hospital analysts, in contrast to their previous approach, which relied on rarely codified anecdotal evidence, interviewed staff and physicians, much as medical-device and pharmaceutical sales forces commonly do. Learning how rival hospitals influence physician referrals offered insights that helped develop countermeasures to gain market share. Hospital administrators responsible for building relationships with physicians started reaching out to them, and the hospital enhanced its continuing medical-education programs for certain strategic service lines. In addition, a revamping of the Web site, direct-mail system, and advertisements of the hospital raised awareness of it both among referring doctors and prospective patients.

Well-prepared hospitals evaluate the growth potential not just of initial care episodes in a given clinical area but also of related services. To do so, they must understand how patients typically flow within and between service lines. Such an understanding requires hospitals to study disease pathways, likely treatment regimens, and relevant treatment technologies. For example, along with a local physician group, the hospital then invested in a heart failure clinic and began making more regular contact with patients. It turned out that many of congestive heart failure patients could benefit from device therapy (such as implanted defibrillators or ventricular resynchronization). The hospital's focus on its long-term relationship with heart failure patients was critical to its success. Just as retailers and financial-services companies use customer data to their advantage in building enduring relationships, providers increasingly recognize the value of advanced customer-relationship-management techniques. When and where changes are necessary Identifying the most competitive service lines is only half the battle; hospitals also need to change the way they operate these service lines. Rewards for success can be substantial. For example, one hospital have purchased many new medical equipment, if it increased its annual profits by about $15 million within two years of undertaking an ambitious service-line reorientation. I believe that its medical equipment can let many surgeon patients feel medical service satisfaction.

- Effective time management performance measurement

Changing people processes Implementing a service-line strategy requires changing how a hospital manages human resources. Hospitals may need to recruit more people for critical service lines and fewer for others. Not least important, the professionals and staff of each service line must understand the new strategy and accept the plan so that they will be willing to change the way they work. Incentives that encourage the staff, particularly physicians, to act like owners—including more formal joint-ownership structures, such as equity sharing, investment partnerships, or even full employment—are typically necessary to align the physicians' interests with those of the hospital.

When on hospital changed its personnel processes to support its advanced cardiovascular service line and its elective general-surgery program, which focused on breast cancer. The hospital filled talent gaps by recruiting new physicians (including, for instance, a radiologist with experience and interest in mammography) and increased training to ensure the clinical competency of the operating-room support staff. Before updating an existing joint business plan to improve the alignment between the new goals and the interests of the relevant specialists, the hospital conducted extensive conversations with them. Measuring progress When it comes to performance, most hospitals track only gross patient volumes, net revenue, and, sometimes, hospital-wide profit margins. But to ensure that a service-line strategy is working, they must also track patient-level performance.
For every patient admitted and diagnosed, a hospital might assign a score indicating the clinical outcome and monitor both the cost to treat the patient and the patient's total charges. These cost-accounting figures, plus yields from managed-care contracts, are vital to tracking a hospital's progress. Furthermore, because service-line strategies may take years to implement and show results, it is important to track process milestones (such as the recruitment of key physicians) and traditional measures such as profit margins or the total volume of cases. Like many hospitals, Springfield

General found that quarterly performance scorecards helped it track both its financial and nonfinancial performance at a greater level of detail than had previously been possible.

Measuring performance with this degree of precision is challenging, so hospitals should consider taking interim steps. A hospital might use the ratio of costs to charges from each department to gauge a service line's performance. Knowing how every patient is admitted (through the emergency department, electively, or by referral from a specific physician group) can help the hospital to uncover patterns of unusually high or low profitability or possible sources of additional volume.

In addition, tracking how much a hospital actually collects for a service line (after writing off bad debt) can help to judge its true profitability and inform future contract negotiations with payers.An added benefit of detailed performance metrics is that their use often generates a virtuous cycle of improved clinical outcomes. Hospitals should track outcome-specific patient-level data (for example, the time from the arrival of a postsurgery coronary-bypass patient in the intensive-care unit to the point when the patient no longer needs the help of a ventilator to breathe) rather than more generic measures (such as whether discharge instructions were delivered). The more specific approach allows hospitals both to pinpoint areas of care that need improvement and to reward effective performance by the administrative, managerial, and clinical staff.

Managing service lines that aren't a priority In most cases, service lines that are not a strategic priority will continue operating at some level to help hospitals meet basic community needs and cover fixed costs. Hospitals should avoid investing large amounts of capital, their physicians' management time, or executive leadership in nonpriority service lines. But such clinical areas often employ dedicated nursing staff, support personnel, and physicians, most of whom have a vested interest in the status quo. Hospital leaders must develop an effective communication plan to lay out the rationale for change and to set the staff's expectations. The hospital should tell its employees that it will maintain high safety and quality standards but probably won't be an early adopter of expensive technologies in these service lines and won't respond to competitive forces.

For the emergency department, when the hospital choose to limit capital investments, marketing budgets, and efforts to reach previously unaffiliated physicians, as well as to reallocate a portion of the department's expanded space to a gastrointestinal diagnostics unit. The initial reaction of the emergency department's physicians was predictably negative, but by communicating the strategy effectively and sharing the data underlying the decision-making process, the administrative team eventually gained the confidence of the medical professionals, including those in the emergency department. It also used this transparent approach to reassure the broader community that the new strategy was in its best interest as well. Although the emergency department was scaled back, the community benefited from expanded colorectal-cancer-screening outreach programs and gastrointestinal-disease seminars for both the public and the primary-care community. So, emergency department medical equipment need is essential to any hospital service improvement if the hospital hopes to innovate its medical service to let any emergency service patients feel satisfactory.

● What 4 Factors Should Determine a Hospital's Service Line Strategy?

These include the hospital's mission, market growth, margin and the likelihood of the service line's success, as well as the following factors:

• Hospital mission: Type of patient care (secondary, tertiary, quaternary); types of education; and types of research.

• Market growth: Growth by service line; payor mix by service line; ability to feed into other key profitable service lines; and the ability to partner with payors and/or employers and shift share.

• Margin: Payor mix by service line; impact of reimbursement changes; and ability to partner with physicians to control costs.

• Likelihood of success: Necessary investments, such as physician recruitment and capital expenditures; internal capabilities; and competitors' capabilities.

The rate at which these lines are expected to grow is not directly correlated with their profitability, however. For instance, out of those five specialties, orthopedics is generally third in terms of profits and General surgery is the most profitable. Hospitals will need to cross-examine each specialty's expected market growth and its profitability, as service lines across hospitals and geographies can present different clusters of performance. While this data can help hospitals prioritize their service lines, some qualitative factors also need consideration, such as competitors' capabilities. Do competitors offer any specific services within their service line? Do they provide key feeder services for your hospital? Also, what is physicians' perception of competitors? How aggressively do they market their service lines? These questions can help bring a greater understanding to how likely a hospital service line is to succeed.

CHAPTER FOUR

SCHOOL TIME MANAGEMENT

What are the factors which can influence the final grades of academic students ? I shall indicate as below:

- Tutoring teaching time management

influences student learning behavior

The tutoring method factor includes self-determined tutoring, academic advisor schedules tutoring, group tutoring, one-to-one tutoring, peer tutoring and professional tutoring. These different kinds of tutoring method can influence the final grades to any academic student. As the cognitive learning theory and humanistic theory both are for this study conceptual framework. The results of a one-way analysis of variance determined there were significant differences in final grades of students who received group tutoring compared to one-to-one tutoring and peer tutoring compared to professional tutoring.

In fact, many colleges and universities have had to provide tutoring to attend to the needs of all students' aims to teach them how to write assignments and how to exam to get higher grades. However, any methods of a tutoring will have benefits and weakness to any students. For example, students who attend group tutoring may have an advantage because other students may contribute additional information relevant to questions, whereas one-to-one tutoring will give the students the undivided attention of the tutor. In addition, students who attend tutoring provided by their peers rather than professonal tutors may feel more relaxed and relate to them differently then professional helpers. What methods do tutors use? Tutoring methods usually include self-determined, academic advisor, determined programs group, one-to-one, peer and professional tutoring. What is the relationship between final grades and tutoring programs. I suggested that academic programs, particularly professional tutoring are successful and may lead to increase student persistence in course completion. In fact, students who activity participated in the tutoring program had greater academic success compared to those who did not participate in the tutoring program. Further, no researchers had compared outcomes for students who received tutoring in a group setting rather than one-to-one settings.

In addition, no researchers had compared outcomes for students who receive tutoring from peer tutors rather than professional tutors. Also no research was found that outcomes were for students who were required to participate in tutoring services, but allowed to self-determine that schedules. However, research has shown that students who voluntary received tutoring service regularly most often received a passing grade in the course for which who received tutoring.

- learning time management motivation factor

Reading habits are well planned of study which has attained a form of consistency on the part of students towards understanding academic subjects and passing at examinations. Both reading and academic achievements are interrelated and dependent on each other. Reading habits involve personal investigation, self-study, self thinking and analysis to each bok's content. So, reading habit is the student himself/herself motivation, it is not motivated by teachers, who need to spend their leisure time in reading both English and literature. However, the problem most students have that contributes to their poor performance in tests and examinations is lack of proper reading habits. For an excellent performance, there is the need to the student to form good reading and study habits. Whether what are the reading habits among students? Has reading habit effect on academic performance? Is there a relationship between student's reading habits and academic performance? What kind of materials to students read when who visit the library? Why do students engage in reading? People read for different reasons and purposes, some of which include for pleasure, leisure, relaxation and for knowledge.

In student view point, reading is an essential tool for knowledge transfer and the habit of reading is academic activity that increases skills in reading strategies. It seems reading habit can help any student to raise knowledge and writing ability to prepare to write their assignments for those different subjects and examinations. It is possible that examination grades and study habit has close relationship.

- Classroom time management

The major reasons are given by students for non-attendance which include external influences of assessment pressures, poor delivery of lecturers, timing of lectures and work commitments and financial constraints. Indeed, web-based learning approaches have become popular instead of some classroom attendance universities in our societies. So, it causes students who don't need to attend to classroom regularly. Although, some existing evidence points to a strong correlation between attendance and academic performance, no effect of the studies citied above demonstrate a causal affect. However, the levels of motivation, intelligence, prior learning and time-management skills is a major limiting factor to the utility of causal affect. However, these relationships are contingent upon a number of factors, such that it is nearly impossible to predict academic performance using socio-economic. To conclude, the non-attendance or attendance factor influences academic performance is difficult to measure, such as student motivation, socio-economic status and attendance is required to influence why the student choose to attend or not attend the classrooms.

The conclusion to drawn from this study is that gender, age, learning preference and entry qualifications did not cause any significant variation in the academic performance of students. Although, some students' academic performance were not significantly different from the rest of the students. It seems some talent students who don't need to attend any classrooms and their non-attendance behaviors won't influence their academic performance to be bad. Otherwise, some foolish students who need to attend classrooms to achieve passing grades.

Whether academic motivation can be a mediator for achievement. It was hypothesized that heavy drinking decreases academic motivation, which subsequently also decreases academic achievement. The effects of drinking on univerity grades: Does academic motivation play a role? However, academic achievement can be influenced by a number of factors and the effect of alcohol consumption on achievement has been of particular interest to researcher. Heavy drinking habit of students, e.g. weekly drinking alcohol, and/or consumption six or more alcohol on each occasion of drinking, these heavy drinking alcohol behaviour can influence these drinking wine students whose grades to be gone down in possible. High drinking wine or alcohol habit can cause day time sleepiness, unhealthy behaviours, like unhealthy sleep patterns because they may be linked to behavioural consequences. Due to students who regularly drink alchohol, then whose drinking behaviours have interrupted sleep cycles: They go to bed late, wake up late and experience increased daytime sleepiness. All factors of which were found to be associated with decreased academic performance. It seems heavy drinking alcohol habit of intelligent students will get the bad academic performance also.

● The relationship between physical fitness
and learning time arrangement

Whether has it close relationship to link unhealthy sleep habits and academic performance. Such as current study examined the relationship between grade point average (GPA) and sleep, in terms of quality and quantity. In general, human need have four different aspects of sleep quantity. These aspect included number of nights spent with less than five hours of sleep during the past week, as well as during an average week, number of hours of sleep obtained in an average night, as well as the number of all nighter's the students. Results indicated a significant positive correlation between amount of sleep per night with GPA, and a significant negative correlation between average number of day per week that students obtained less than five hours of sleep and GPA.

Health sleep habits can defined , such as self-rated satisfaction with sleep, enough sleeping during the night non difficulty sleeping at night and non over sleeping. If students are unsatisfied with their quality of sleep, who will encounter studying problems, due to who lack nervous to attend any classrooms to listen any lecturers' speaking to remember any important contents of their different subjects every day. So, their non sleeping bad behaviour which will cause them to get the bad academic performance in possible finally.

● The relationship between physical fitness
and learning time arrangement

Whether can lacking enough physical fitness sport cause students to get bad academic performance? In fact, human needs health physical ftness of life to carrying on working or studying. Physical movements of the body are vital for normal brain development to children or young adult. So if the child or young adult chooses to spend whose time to often play video games to watch television or occupies himself/herself on the computer on the weekends and after school, instead of any physical fitness sports in whose relax time to spend time to do. It will have chance to cause blood pressure, depression and other diseases to him or her. It seems any student ought have enough time to do physical fitness to keep him or her mental health benefit to prepare to have health body to learn. Otherwise, lacking physical activity will cause lower levels of self-esteem and lower levels of anxiety to cause lower academic performance in the classroom to any students. For example, the mathematics and science students who need have health body to go to classroom to study. So, enough physical sports activities are important to these students. Due to a more focused mindset on academic performance has hindered the quality and quantity of these mathematics and science students to learn in classroom everyday. So, physical fitness has close relationship to academic performance.

The student's personal factor, such as level of motivation, persistence, responsibility and need for structure, whether these factors can can influence whose academic performance. Which is learning style? It is the way a person processes, internalizes and studies new and challenging material. Student's performance may be related to learning preferences or styles as learners. Some experiments indicates that college students taught in their preferred learning styles scores higher on tests, fact knowledge, attitude and efficiency than those taught in instructional style. So mismatch of teaching styles and learning styles could give negative impaxt to students. In the psychological view, due to students tend to be bored on inattentive in class, do poorly on tests, get discouraged about the course and may conclude that who are not good in the subject. As a result, students' success in classes may depend an understanding the learning style characteristics of students who enrol in the respective courses.

● The relationship between teaching time management and private time management

Managing time is any student's responsibilities. Time management is a skill that every student should not only know, but also apply. A lot of university students complain about running out of time when who need to do a certain assignment or prepare examination. They get frustrated beause who are not able to finish it before the due date. On the other hand, they spend a lot of time to meet their friends or playing, so who have no enough time to enhance their learning of productivity in order to get low grades. For example, a subject assignment needs have a important due date to finish to submit because who lack time management skill to predict the size of assignment, who need how long time to finish. So they won't have enough time to finish the assignment to submit before the due date to cause to get fail grade of the assignment.

In conclusion, any university students ought need to considerate these bad behaviours can influence their final grades. So, you ought to avoid to do these bad behaviours to reduce your bad grades risk occurrence.

Analysis of time factor influencing online reading behavior

Nowadays, online newspapers will be popular to let readers to read any newspapers' news from internet. It showed that for online newspapers reader's intention is influenced by performance expectancy, habit and the habit of reading a print newspapers. So, newspapers consumer personal reading behavior was influenced by intention and habit. Some reading behavioral researchers showed some reasons to explain why traditional paper newspaper readers will like to change habits to study online newspapers.

Hence, changing reading habit will be one factor to influence traditional paper newspaper reader individual reading behavior changes to online newspapers reading habit. In fact, high technological communication media will influence mobile phone and internet both new communication media causes. These new communication medias will bring new print electronic media causes, such as print newspapers, online book products. Some of traditional paper newspaper readers will choose to read any news from online newspapers. The reasons include free charge, reading at home in convenient, not need go out newspapers, online newspapers do not need the reader's hands to touch the black word paper newspaper to be dirty, and waste less time to buy every day to achieve economic benefit.

Every online newspaper reader will have this factor to influence whom to change traditional paper newspaper reading habit. The factor shows that attitude has a direct effect on intentions, and is influenced by performance expectancy and effort expectancy or related personal online reading acceptance conceptions. Because of whose acceptance of online newspaper reading attitude is as an important in technology user online newspaper reading attitude was included.

Additional, every online newspaper reader self-efficacy and anxiety are expected to be minor issue to influence the online newspaper reader to change whose attitude to choose not to internet tool to read of an online newspaper. However, different age reader either he/she is young or old age factor will have influence whom to choose online newspaper to read, e.g. old age readers will feel difficult to apply internet technology to read newspaper, otherwise, young age readers will feel easy to apply internet technology to read newspaper. So, the old or young age traditional paper newspaper readers, when the acceptance new technological online newspaper to them, they will adopt online newspaper reading attitude to replace traditional paper newspaper reading habit more easy. So, their acceptance new technological of online newspaper reading attitude will have a direct effect on online newspaper reading intention and are influenced by both paper and online newspapers reading enjoyment performance expectation and online newspapers reading effort expectation, when their expectations were needed to be satisfied more these past traditional paper newspaper reading experience. Moreover, past paper newspapers reading behavior and habit should be noted. Then, these two expectation factors will encourage or persuade the traditional paper newspaper readers change whose reading attitude, reading habit and reading behavior to read online newspapers. Hence, the online newspaper readers' psychological factor will influence whose traditional paper newspapers readers whose reading behavioral changes. Also, it means that expectation factor will influence the traditional newspaper readers to change whose counter intentional paper newspaper reading habit.

However, online newspaper will bring much knowledge to compare traditional paper newspapers , e.g. real newspapers news data, more meaningfulness news, providing the nature of visiting a news website, which can let online news readers can feel different read model primary on frequency with relatively little spread in the amounts of time spent at the site.

What are the main factors to influence online newspaper reading behaviors? Same testing indicates for moderation by the online newspaper age, gender and online newspaper reading experience will bring the online reading newspapers habit influence. The testing also indicates male gender and young age group , this group likes to apply internet to find or seek or search any news matters. Hence, this internet user group will bring to have interest to read newspapers from internet channel. The reason is possible because this young male internet users like to contact new technology, e.g. internet. They think the online newspaper is useful and it is more useful to read the online newspaper to compare to paper newspaper.

The two reasons : liking to contact new technology and feeling the online newspaper is more useful which can support why young male online internet users feel to expect reading online newspaper expectancy were more concrete.

Additional online newspapers usefulness are more considered on unclear concept to explain why this reader group feels more like to study online newspapers. What exactly is the usefulness of reading an online newspaper?

The testing also indicated that some online newspaper readers responded to use the online newspaper to feel natural, it showed to be related to attitude as well as to habit , which seems to hold face validity as a natural feel can be considered on attitude on the online newspaper. So, online reading attitude and online reading habit can reflect why man young male like to read online newspapers more than paper newspaper reason.

Another reason indicated that when the young male readers want to read the news, the online newspaper is an obvious choice for him/her. So, many online newspaper young male readers had felt online newspaper is one another newspaper reading choice to replace traditional paper newspapers.

In conclusion , free charge online newspaper is not the main factor to influence both traditional paper newspaper readers to change their reading habit to choose online newspapers to read suddenly. There are other factors to cause them to choose online newspapers to read, such as more usefulness feeling, contacting new technology, online reading habit, positive online reading attitude etc. different psychological factors which will have more influences to cause their paper newspaper reading habits to be changed. Hence, the free price economic gain actor must not only one main factor to persuade readers to choose online newspapers to read.

- How time factor influences electronic versus traditional print textbook influence of university students' learning behavior in school

When one university student was accepted by
electronic text book learning channel to replace traditional paper text book learning channel (methods). Electronic text book will bring what positive or/and negative influence to impact whose learning behavior changes. For example, electronic text book learning method will bring positive impact to raise the student's examination grades and perceived learning scores or it will bring negative impact to fall down the student's examination grades and perceived learning scores. The mean scores indicated that students who choose to text books for their learning aim. It will have significantly higher perceived affective learning performance and examination results. Thus, the purpose of student learning and teacher teaching method, every

university needs to examine whether it is efficient to raise student learning effort to replace paper text book learning method in any learning environment, e.g. many students and one teacher classroom learning environment or the independent student learns himself/herself at home learning environment or library learning environment.

Can text book reading tool bring absolute advantages to university students or bring some disadvantages to them? When a student needs to apply e-text book to learn, who needs access e-text book in a static location, such as a computer or on a mobile device. So, the e-text book in a static location factor, it will have influence to each student reading or learning behavior to bring negative and/or positive both impacts.

The e-text book was distributed on a CD and installed on a located computer. This limited the user to accessing the e-textbook in a single location and eliminated the potential access to the e-text book on due to the lack of mobility. So, it seems that the location of limited to e-text book will bring negative impact to let the student can only learn in a fixed location because he/she will feel difficult to move heavy computer to other places to learn more than on paper text book. So, e-text book location can not allow the student to leave the classroom to learn more easier if he/she had chose to use to computer to install the CD to learn in the classroom. Supposing the student 's teacher needs the student often to leave the classroom to discuss any matter suddenly, it is not very convenient to the student to use e-text book to learn because he/she can not move the computer to leave the classroom with him/her easily. Then, it will be possible to influence the student can bot be attention to read the e-text book, when the teacher needs the student to leave the classroom (none book bringing) to discuss any time any time immediately. Otherwise, if the student used one paper book to read/learn in the classroom, if the teacher needs whom to leave the classroom often to discuss immediately. He/she will feel convenient to learn because he/she can bring the light paper book to leave the classroom to discuss with the teacher in any location easily.

Hence, it seems e-text book learning will bring not convenient fixed location learning environment to every e-texting learning student in classroom, when, he/she needs often to leave the classroom to discuss with the teacher any time.

Other disadvantage of e-text learning will bring students feel difficult in possible. In the past, some learning researcher experiments indicated results demonstrated that student participants in both groups had similar recall and ability to reinterpret information suggesting that retrieval of information is not effected by kindle e-book reader e-text book, a tabled computer e-text book or a print version.

Hence, it seems that e-text book can not help or assist recall the student's learning memory to remember the e-text book content more easier. Due to it is one e-text book machine, the student will fell to difficult to find any unclear or important information in any page(s) to write for learning/ reading record more easier than one paper text book.

Another disadvantage of e-text book is the inefficacy or inefficient reading challenge to the e-text book reader. The efficacy of e-text books in a higher education environment will be one interesting discussing question. Passage length is one difference that impact the results. Studies involving shorter reading sessions indicated no substantial variance with respect to reading comprehension and understanding.

Conversely, studies involving longer reading passages indicated prior comprehension, when reading longer e-text , eye fatigue and mental workload are also concerns. Hence, e-text book reading will be possible to let students feel eye fatigue and mental workload in their reading process.

Due to machine e-text book words are more small size and unclear more than paper text book words to print to let students to read every words or sentences in computer. Consequently, studies indicated that e-text book readers need to spend much nervous and time to read longer and poor comprehension in whole e-text book reading process. When, university students need to spend time to read longer e-texts from computers. For example, they need to choose to reads hundreds of papers of e-text books on a screen, whether on a computer or handheld electronic device compared to print versions may contribute to eye fatigue. The consequence, eyestrain and mental fatigue could be poorer comprehension and have a poor eye, nervous health influence and every student's e-text learning behavior can bring negative reading habit to whom, when every one need to apply desktop or laptop or mobile electronic tools to read any words from e-textbooks. Hence, it seems e-text book reading method has possible to bring poor health challenge to every student.

So, above all these e-learning reading factors to bring this question: Does e-learning influence the student's negative reading behavior to cause poor final examination grades results? In fact, every student needs to change whose traditional learning method from paper text book reading habit or reading behavior to e-text books. He/she needs to change whose reading habit. He/she must need to spend long time to accept how to adopt this kind of new technological reading method as well as effect may change through a new technological learning experience itself and impacts the acquisition of knowledge leading to reading behavioral change.

As I indicated the e-learning will bring poor health and poor nervous negative influences when the student often needs to apply electronic product to read long time. So, it will be possible to influence the student health to be poor to bring examination low grades results in possible be cause he/she has poor health to exam.

It is possible that it has relationship to influence the student to exam low grade between e-learning habit and poor health causes. The reason is based on that efficacy of textbook format is defined grades. I assume that all these negative e-text book reading factors can influence every e-text book reader's health to be poor when he/she needs often read e-text book s to cause long time reading habit. So, I mean that e-text book reader individual health changes to poor, it is only depend on how long time e-text book reading habit factor. So, if he/she only spend less time to read e-text books and he/she also has habit to read paper books sometimes. Then, he/she won't be influenced to be poor from e-learning method easily.

It means that it has none direct relationship between less time e-text book reading habit and low examination grades result. Hence, low examination grades result to the student, it only depends on long time e-text book reading habit and the student's long time e-text book reading habit needs to confirm that whose long time e-text book reading habit causes poor health to the student effect. Why do I believe that efficacy of textbook format can influence the student's examination grade? Based on above analysis, the e-text book reading format and paper book reading format is very different. For example, the efficacy of textbook is very different between paper text book reading format and electronic text book reading format. Such as one sickness student needs to spend more nervous to read one e-text book more than one paper text book . This reason is because machine reading method is difficult to compare paper reading method. When the student has sickness, who must need to spend more time and nervous to read one e-text book more than one paper text book. If my assumption is right, then the e-text book sickness reader's reading efficacy to each paper must be poor to compare the paper text book sickness reader , due to the sickness e-text book reader needs to spend long time and much nervous to read each paper more than he/she chooses to read one paper book. When he/she is sickness to finish whose reading . Due to his/her memory will be poor and tries, when he/she feels sick, so whose reading effort must be poor when he/she needs to apply computer tools or mobiles to read.

● How time factor changes future students e-learning habit in school

Nowadays, publishers, internet bookstores manufacturer e-readers have high expectations for digital future of book industry. If they expected e-book publishing industry success, they need to considerate how to assist to future e-readers to let them to feel whose reading habit to be better in order to persuade or attract them to choose to read e-books more easily, due to doctors indicated that long time e-books reading will cause eye poor health and tired and poor nervous reason in possible and paper book price competition and more topic choice reason. It is one value consideration question that e-book publishers need to considerate.

For example, in the US Amazon publish has improved the reading market by producing e Reader that is easy to use and making it easy for clients to purchase a wide variety of books at competitive prices. It will bring digital reader technology as an opportunity to open new target markets and create new e-readers. The question is how Amazon publish , such as e-book publishers change future e-reader reading habit to feel to choose e-books reading method is better than paper books reading method. The successful factors may include as below:

E-book reading market is similar to e-music listening market. They need every e-book reader and/or digital music listen listener to discover why to apply this kind of new digital technology reading or listening method which is better to enjoy to read every e-book content and/or listen every digital music song in order to adopt new listening and/or reading digital technological learning habits or experiences. So, this new digital technological reading or/and digital music listening process, every e-book reader or digital music listener needs to learn how to adopt this kind new digital reading or/and listening products to change from his/her traditional paper book reading or/and CD/DVD music song listening method to this new technological digital reading or listening methods from computer tool channel.

In this changing habit process, every e-book reader or/and e-music listener needs to spend some time to learn how to apply internet technological tool to help whose to read digital book or listen digital music from computer channel. So, he/she must attempt to change whose habit from traditional paper book reading habit and/or CD/DVD listening music habit to e-book reading habit and/or e-music listening habit.

Furthermore, e-book publishers also need to know whether which kind of book topics are be favorable popular to be chose to read for either student reader target to read or mature age reader target to read or old age reader target to read. Who will purchase the topic to read to be e-Reader? Will they be designed to appeal to be a group of e-reader customers or only to those who have a high degree of comfort with technology to enjoy e-reading method? Will people who read once in a time be purchased by the small group of e-reading clients who buy and read a high volume of e-books? What reasons, readers will choose to read the topics of e-books more than paper books? Will publishers be able to use e-books and e-readers to extend the many different age e-reading clients, e.g. young, mature, retirement, old, student age e-readers? Will publishers ever more to all readers are only choose digital e-reading model habit or who are a half digital e-reader and a half paper book reading habit clients to them?

Hence, one successful digital publisher needs to consider how to persuade every traditional paper book habit readers to change their reading habit to read digital e-books from computer. Because changing habit is one challenge to influence the e-book publisher 's e-book reader number. How to persuade the paper book reading habit readers to change whose attitude to choose to read e-books , it is one considerate question to every digital publisher? Some readers may feel difficult that who needs to learn new knowledge how to read e-books from computer tool, e.g. old age reader group. This reason will influence they still choose paper books to read in habit. So, any e-book publisher has responsibility to teach new digital technological knowledge learning method to let the e-book desire readers can feel easy to apply internet to read e-books from computer tool.

Another factor is e-book price, normally every e-book price will need to be sold cheaper to compare the similar paper book topic in order to persuade paper book readers choose to buy the similar topic of e-books to read more easily. Because if the reader discover the e-book topic is similar to the paper book topic contents, but the e-book price is charged high than the similar paper book topic content, then he/she will possible to choose to buy the similar paper book topic to read.

Another factor concerns how to raise e-books attraction. E-publishers will need to position themselves as content providers, and not just to be similar to the suppliers of physical books. They will have to make content available on multiple media, in multiple formats, on multiple platforms. This content may not be limited to the text of a digital book itself, it may also include audio, video, image and sound speaking digital books to attract e-readers' attention.

Another factor is that I recommend e-book publishers need to let all e-book readers to feel reading e-books are leisure time habit to let them to enjoy life every day in popular. Intention is such as good tool for anyone to apply to entertainment, for example people linked using internet to read books, watch movies, play video games from computer tool. They are some main points. They have same main points. They tend to spend leisure time with electronic media, such as apply internet to watch television which is such as to apply internet one more choice to assist readers to read e-books from computer media tool conveniently at home.

However, this is one example e-book attraction point to e-reader. Every e-book needs have e-pub files to allow readers to control the size of the text or their computer screens. If the e-reader feels the text is small size and computer screen is small size in difficult to read. Then, he/she can use mouse tool to change the e-book text number to be high number, e.g. from 18 to 20 or more number and he/she can apply mouse tool to move the computer screen to be wider more easily. Hence, it is e-book attraction point to e-book readers to feel when he/she feel the text is small size to read in difficult. Otherwise, every paper book print text(word) size is fixed, all word size can not be changed to read and every paper book wide size is also fixed. All it is every paper's unattraction point to every paper book reader.

Consequently, every e-book publisher needs have its attraction point to let its every e-book reader feels it is different to the other paper book publishers. It needs to solve these challenges to let its every reader to accept to choose its e-book reading channel. The challenges may include how to let the e-reader feels its e-book reading media can provide a more comfortable e-reading experience to compare other e-book publishers' reading media, how to let its e-readers feels its all e-books can provide one precise and stable e-book reading characteristics, how to let its ebook readers to feel its every ebook displays does not require any background lighting and one easy to read, even in direct sunlight environment, and it e-reading tool can spend less energy from laptop battery or desktop electricity to compare other e-book publisher reading tool, it means that the e-book publisher's ebook reading tool can provide a recharged power desire which can be used for several thousand pages or seveal weeks e-reading function. Hence, it the e-book publisher's e-book reading tool can provide more clear words and text image as well as less electricity consumption function to let every e-reader to read to compare other ebook publishers from laptop, destop or mobile media. Then , the ebook publisher's competitive effort will raise to win its other ebook publishing competitors. However, any ebook publisher needs have attraction points to persuade its ebook readers to read its any ebooks feel comfortable and providing fun ebooks choices and easy to read its every ebook text more clear if it expects to win its competitors in ebook publishing industry.

Reading failure is a serious educational problem to influence every publisher success because if the child chooses to buy its books to read, but its child readers can not feel its books can help them to assist their learning success or failure examination or low grades result. Then, it will influence its child reader number to be reduced. However, the factors cause reading failure, it is not only considered to the publisher's poor book content quality factor, it can include the other factors such as: It is simply be attributed by poverty, immigration or the learning of English as a second language. What factors will influence child read in wrong habit to bring reading failure, even learning failure in effect? It is one question to every publisher needs to know in order to avoid they feel failure examination emotion after read their e-text books. Hence, how to design every text book content is one important issue to ever publisher.

A study by Yankelovich found most children are reading, but they are not reading enough. It indicated only about 3 in 10 children can be classified as high frequency readers who read books for fun ever day. Age 8 children are less to see benefits t oreading for fun, girls are more likely boys to have positive attitude about reading and feel fun. The benefits of reading are evidenced by the attitude of high frequency readers to achieve future learng success. More than 40% of children ages 5 to 8 say they are high frequency readers, by ages 9 to 11 that proportation drops to 29%. Almost half of the 15 to 17 year old (46%) are low frequency readers compared with 14% of 5 to 8 year old age. So, this study investigation reflected that building good learning habit has relationship between frequency reading and feeling fun to read to every child. It seems that one fun content book can attract the child to read the whole book all content really. So, publisher needs to consider how to design and write attractive content books to let every child to read.

What factors cause every child feel barriers to read? Some investigations indicate that young children tend to maintain high expectations for success, even in the face of regarded failure, when old students don't, also to older students feel failure following high effort appears to carry more negative inplications. Moreover, all students individual attitude about their capabilities and their interpretation of success and failure is further factor to affect their willingness to feel fun to read in themselves learning proceses.

So, it concludes this fun book content design method can persuade young people feel fun to read really. Moviated readers hold positive benefits about themselves attitude or reading habit which will bring positive and attractive reading emotion to influence them.

What are the book publishers and teachers' responsibilities to improve student individual negative habit to have positive reading habit or positive learning attitude? The ultimate goal in teaching and reading book is to raise students comprehend te ideas in a piece of text as they need. So, any publisher has responsibility to publish one fun and meaning book in prior, because every teacher will teach whose students by the text book content. If the text book content is fun and attractive and meaning, then the teacher can teach to let every students to learn more easily.

Training every student owns good reading habit which can help whom expand their thinking skills, learn to concentrate and enlarge their vocabulary and effectively better their learning environment. The good reading habit ought be trained from the child stage in beginning. So, when the child has is growing up, when he/she is needed to go to primary, secondary, even university to study, he/she had been built good reading habit from the publishers' fun and meaning book content influence in order to let they further learn any new knowledge to feel more easily. So, publishers have responsibilities to sell fun and meaning content books to let every child to read to raise whom reading interest to further young and mature learning stages.

However, the problems, children experience learning to read are often not related to their ability to learn, but to their awareness. Their ability to hear the English language and their expose to the English words. So, repeating to spell the English words will assist the child to raise memory to remember to write the English words more easily. So, book publishers have responsibilities to express every book content to attact child readers to feel interest or fun to learn to remember to spell every word as well as teachers have responsibilities to train students how to hear the words, he/she assist every child to learn to spell the English word more easily. So, teachers ought often speak every word or speak every sentence loudly from every book content to let students to listen easily in order to let they can raise every word memory more easily.

Consequently, instead of child's parents and child himself/herslf has responsibility to help the child self to build good reading habit, teachers and book publishers have also responsibilities to help them to build good reading habit because fun and meaningful books which bring more attraction to influence every child to read, when the book is fun and meaningful , then the teacher can follow its content to teach whose students to attract them to learn more easily. However, the good reading habit includes elements of reading comprehension to every book content , such as: identifying and summarizing the main idea, comparing and contrasting, identifying supporting facts and details, making influences and drawing conclusions, predicting outcomes, recognizing fact and opinion, identigy cause and effect recognizing sequence of events, identifying story / case elemetnts, such as main characters, settings, conflict, and resolution, identifying the another's purpiose and point of view, interpreting literary devices, such as imagery , symbolisms.

Hence, publishers ought to follow above these elements to design their every book content in order to let child readers to feel fun and meaningful and easy to read. Because reading comprehension elements will be one important factor to train every child or mature student reader to build good reading habit or attitude more easily and effectively in order to raise their future good reading effort in their every learning stage in success.

CHAPTER FIVE

A national chain of restaurant mobile advertising time management

Critically assess the likely opportunities and problems
of mobile advertising for a national chain of restaurants in short time yahoo web mobile advertise

Can short time mobile restaurant advertise persuade travellers to choose the restaurant in preference , when they see the restaurant advertise to let them to know the different meal price and kinds of meal choice and location in the only ten minutes short advertise message from yahoo web channel every day? Usuall, mobile users will turn on short time and they also control their mobile turning on time in their time control. Such as turning on mobile on non-working hours, so they only turn on mobiles on lunch time or finishing work or going back home time. So, a national chain of restaurant needs to arrange its advertise time to let they turn on their mobiles to see their meal advestaurant from yahoo web. So, effective advertise time arrangement is very important to let them to know their restaurant advertise. Moreover, their mobile advertise can not be too long and it have advertise time limit, e.g. every day , it only advertise its restaurant advertise 10 minutes from yahoo web. So, it will attract the first time mobile users' interest to know whether it will provide what kind of eating service , if they feel difficult to know whether what kind of eating service , that it can provide on the first time adverise message within the 10 minute mobile advertise on that day. Then, they will hope it can advertise its advertise to let them may know more concerns its eating service message when they turn on their mobile again next day. So, mobile advertise time mangement will be important to raise any restaurant eatting customers' interest when they are the first time to contact this restaurant's advertise.

A global crisis in the advertising industry largely linked to the impact of the internet is transforming the business models of media industries, the content they create and distribute, and the audiences who consume that contents. Such as consumers can use whose mobiles to find where the chain of restaurants are located and meal and drink prices and meal and drink types and
restaurant opening and closing time etc. information for the national chain of restaurants from internet advertising when who leave at home conveniently. The opportunity to mobile advertising for a national chain of restaurants, it can expand its national chain of restaurants brand to different countries visitors and instead of its self country visitors to let them to know whether where its chain of restaurants can provide what kinds of food or drink to serve to them to eat before they prepare to go to any one of the national chain of restaurants immediately. Hence, when visitors travel to its country, it will be more easy to let them to remember where any one of the national chain restaurants are located in the nation when who enter the national chain restaurants website or enter yahoo website to type" national chain restaurants" word, then who can seek any one of the national chain restaurants from whose mobiles easily.

In fact, if a national chain of restaurants chose to use television advertising, due to the national chain of restaurants which locate at itself country locally. It is only concentrate on promoting it's country's domestic eating consumers target to know it's existence when its country's domestic eating consumers are watching television at homes. Usually, working people need to work and students need to go to school to study from morning 9:00AM to 6:00 PM at night. Hence, the national chain of restaurants can only advertise at night time. Furthermore, the overseas travelers watch the nation's television when who are staying in the nation's hotels at night time. Hence, the national chain of restaurants can only use television to advertise to attract the largest numbers of local and foreign visitors to watch its advertisement at night time possibly.

Due to mobile advertising exists, television advertising is more difficult to attract the durability of audience segmentation models to build upon demographic and it also lacks new opportunities to implement psychographic and behavioral models for understanding audiences. Such as, many young people who accept to use mobile to communicate, so it implies every family usually has a mobile to use and mobile advertising also have much opportunity to help any businesses to promote whose services or products to let many families to know whose advertising. In fact, mobile users can use mobile to watch movies or news, so who ought to link internet to watch during who are sitting on any transportations or walking, so when the nation's people who feel hungry, who can use their mobiles to link to internet to seek any restaurants to decide which restaurants are the most close to their locations to choose.

As a national chain of restaurants, it is more effective to advertise it's different chain of restaurants' locations to let any it's different locations of national mobile users to seek its any one of chain restaurant conveniently when who are walking on the street if who feel hungry who can turn on mobile to find map to seek the national chain of restaurants immediately. In fact, the global households who the average viewing audience composition, the number of global households using the television set and the various times it is in use, the average audience (home viewing during an average minute of a program) and the total audiences (homes viewing the program in excess of minutes) which are decreasing. Otherwise, the mobile phone users view mobile advertising numbers are increasing. Broadcast channels as well as whatever is available on their various devices, including computer, mobile devices, gaming devices, time-shifting devices or internet enables devices. As such, it is providing more and more difficult to track the audience and known who they are and the best way to target them. Additionally, the rise of social media adds another dimension to audience research. Social media provides new ways of segmenting audiences that currently can not be done on television. Hence, a national chain of restaurants can get better ways of segmenting its viewers from mobile advertising over a variety of platforms.

So mobile networks can be better package to the nation chain of restaurants advertising programming and the national chain of restaurants advertiser can make a more effective to attract foreign visitors or domestic visitors to make them to enter its website to view its advertising from their mobiles. For example, car owners, such as those who own a BMW or Audi famous brands cars, which have very homogeneous demographic characteristics, but each car brand has a specific type of owner with a unique personality. A similar look as television audiences could allow advertising of those car brands (who attend the upfront presentations every year) to match their car buyers to specific television shows. Demographics have not caught up with these changes and presume that viewers are still watching in only the conventional way. For instance, there is not yet a way for the networks to get credit for online viewers and it is as more viewers more to online platforms, like a network in landing site.

Instead, a psychographic profile of the audience, one based on psychological segmentations , such as behaviors, attitudes, interests, values, opinions feelings which is a valid and valuable way of narrowing down the audience into segments for an advertiser. So, psychographic data can measure, such as peoples' activities how who spend whose time, their interests what they place importance on in their immediate surroundings, their opinions how their view of themselves and the world around them and some basic characteristics, such as their stage life cycle and income and education and residence location. The result of the research then provides a detailed profile that allows the marketer to be better visualize the target audience.

Psychographics start with people and reveal how the people feel client specific subjects, which can lead to be more effective marketing. When psychographic segmentations are used, the consumers are divided into group based on lifestyle and personality, often with all of this in mind, the research questions proposed here as follows:

What psychographic measurements are being used right now to determine the television audience or mobile advertising ?

How are the various branches of the industry , such as restaurant industry adaptive to the new television landscape ,such as mobile advertising and what actions are they taking?

What are some challenges and resistances to psychographic measures between television advertising and mobile advertising?

What incentives or lack are there to change between television and mobile advertising?

What would be helpful for advertisers , such as a national chain of restaurants or networks , such as internet advertising to know or do in order to more towards wider use of psychographics?

A reason behind dividing audiences based on engagement can be illustrated with the Pod mobile phone, such as the national chain of restaurants organization has shown that audiences‘ attachment to specific the restaurants' brand corresponds directly to how much the audience will pay attention to the national restaurant brand's advertisements from mobile and how likely who are the actually to choose to go to the national chain of restaurants to eat lunch or dinner or breakfast more than its other restaurants.

The problem is how the national chain of restaurants to advertise it's foods taste, price and service and locations uniquely to win its other restaurant competitors from mobile specific program, providing the network to be best convenient that it's restaurant brand to advertise on that specific program. Another key problem is trend segments viewers based on domestic and foreign consumers' behavior are more specifically their viewing behavior mixed with their restaurants choosing eating behavior in whose countries, watching the national chain of restaurants television advertising from whose mobile , what who are watching to know its existence and on how to let them to know what their actual eating taste to the national chain of restaurants can provide. Hence, I suggest the national chain of restaurants can attempt to use surveys to carry on researching the different countries foreign visitors and domestic visitors whether what whose tastes are preferable to choose what kinds of foods and drinks who hope to eat in this national chain of restaurants from mobile advertising website. The problem is who may choose not to fill its surveys from its mobile website advertising. If they use computer to fill its surveys at home, it will have more opportunities to gather data from survey due to who can sit down to fill surveys in quiet environment. Hence, I suggest it ought use computer internet to do market research about what whose tastes are preferable to eat in its restaurants. When it estimates whether the foreign visitors and domestic visitors numbers, how many people choose to eat different kinds of foods and drinks to its identifications. After it can achieve mobile advertising to promote its restaurant brand more confidently in this mobile marketing advertising strategy.

2. Discuss short time limit mobile advertise message that could be used to assess the effectiveness of mobile advertising.

Measuring social media marketing , such as mobile advertisement, effectiveness and identifying the target market. The use of social media sites as part of company's marketing strategy has increased significantly. Regardless its popularity, there is still very limited information to answer some of the key issues concerning the effectiveness of social media marketing , ways to measure its return on investment and its target market. The social media was started around ten years ago. It began with linked in, which was launched in 2003 year, followed by both My space and face book in 2004 year. You tube in 2005 year and Twitter in 2006 in year.

The popularity of social media sites has also spread to companies as part of their strategies. Executives are concerned with their budget justification for a social media plan in computer or media online advertising, when there is lack of supporting materials to confirm the effectiveness of the social media platform , i.e. conversion rate, the relation between buyer-seller relationship and increase in sales and the rate of return investment that they can earn from this plan. Others also believe that their companies' performance are not affected by their lack of involvement in the social media sites.

Clearly, the fact that social media marketing is still relatively new among business practitioners has raised some major concerns , such as its effectiveness, the main purpose of including social media mobile advertising in a company's media platforms, it's relation to the existing platforms and the target audience of this strategy. The methods to assess effectiveness of mobile advertisement include that marketing research method is about target client segment of respondents' social media activities and buying decisions relationship survey. Survey questions can include whether how long time and how often who turn on mobile phone to use internet, such as a week is less than 20 hours average or a week is between 20 hours and 30 hours average or a week is between 30 hours and 50 hours or a week is more than 50 hours, why who like to use mobile to use internet and not use home computer to use internet, e.g. reducing to use home electricity, interesting, convenience, no computer at home, what who will seek to see from mobile advertisement, e.g. advertisement , news ,email , message, movie, whether who decide to buy products or consume services choice is from which kinds of channel advertisement influence mostly, such as television, radios, newspapers, magazines, computer internet, mobile internet. It aims to gather target client segment of respondents' social media activities and buying decision relationship to estimate whether there are how many numbers of target client will decide to buy the company's product or use it's service from mobile advertisement channel.

Hence, the survey result can indicate these five respondent groups, such as highly affected, somewhat affected, neutral somewhat not affected and not affected at all groups. Mobile phone advertisement is needed to any organizations to use internet to operate. Hence, to access the effectiveness of mobile advertising which may begin by using measures that were very easy to capture and understand, such as the number of website hits or percentage of users who clicked on an advertisement. These measures were very useful fro examining trends in traffic patterns, but the impact of this traffic on sale and other marketing objective was sales and other marketing objectives were little understand. Standardized approaches for capturing and summarizing websites behavior were eventually developed to help make sense of web traffic and patterns. Metrics, such as number of unique visitors and the amount of time who spent viewing web pages provided marketers with new insights into who was assessing the site and how who were using it. But even with a high level of detail about how customers were interacting with the company via the web, marketing manager often lacked the information how user behavior data translates into increased profits and business value. For example, organizations using websites primarily for after sales support have used exactly the same kinds of metrics as these selling directly from the site. This is not due to a lack of available data. Many organizations using web analytics gather and store vast amounts of information and develop large, complex databases to house it. But much of that information is never used. Because organizations who first began to market over the internet often lacked a clearly formulated strategy. In addition, the rapidly changing internet environment made it difficult for marketers to formulate clear expectation about the impact of activities. Both the amount of returns and amount of investments are difficult to measure. I suggest organizations may estimate the value of a visit to a particular web page by estimating the number of visitors who will become customers and then multiplying that number by the average value of all clients to estimate returns. What the 'clicks and hits' and 'measurement driven' approached have in common organization's strategic objectives and provide quantified models that plan and track internet marketing investments from intermediate outcomes to financial results. Hence, it can indicate how marketing expenditures in mobile internet advertising method to lead to increase shareholder value aim. I think investment in internet marketing , organizations will need follow these stages. In the beginning is inputs stage:

Organization and business unit strategy includes structures, systems, resources as well as marketing strategy includes structures, systems as well as information strategy includes structures, systems and market strategy transfers to websites, search marketing , advertisement and public relations, mobile marketing and marketing research. Next, it is outputs stage: It includes intermediate outputs, such as awareness and perceptions, attitudes and intentions, value provisions, channel optimization and market information as well as it includes final outputs, such as marketing assets:

customer value, brand equity, knowledge as well as financial flows: increased revenue, cash flows, reduced revenue, lower cost, lower working capital, lower fixed capital and reduced risk. Finally, it is outcomes stage includes shareholder value, return on investment and corporate profitability. For example, Donald restaurant uses its website to promote lower calorie food and fruit options as well as its global campaign tied to the Olympics, nutrition (Business week 8-7-06). Each organization should carefully identify the outputs it seeks to achieve. How can process produce these outputs? Organization can attempt to enhance of website functional or initiation of an email campaign. The final question to organizations which will ask : How outputs contribute to the long term financial performance of the organization from mobile advertising ?

Is critical for organizations seeking to enhance return on investment from mobile advertising? In addition, whether mobile advertising can give these benefits to any companies, such as market capitalization and shareholder value can be enhanced by increases in marketing assets (customer value, brand equity and knowledge base) that produce future corporate financial flows from mobile internet advertising method. Hence, marketing assets include customer value, such as using dynamic pricing to manage demand, supporting sales through online information sites, shipping directly to reduce need for inventory possession, shifting in store sales to online sales, eliminating clients with prior post sales problems from promotion lists; brand equity, such as additional revenue through brand premiums, using customer relationship to speed adoption of next generation products target marketing to loyal clients during predicted slow periods, reducing customer turnover and support costs, shifting responsibility and risk for inventory management to major suppliers, pool inventories with suppliers and clients to reduce warehouse space across the supply chain, using trust in brand to reduce unwarranted lawsuits, knowledge base, such as developing mass customization capability, reducing time to market through online concept trials, time promotions to smooth demand, eliminating product features that are not valuable to clients. Watching production timing to demand, direct in store sales to products that generate high contribution margin per square foot of fixed space and anticipating and respond to stakeholder concerns. Finally, customer value and brand equity and knowledge base shall transfer to financial flows aim, such as increased revenue, accelerated cash flow, reduced revenue volatility, lower cost, lower working capital requirement, lower fixed capital requirement and reduced risk.

However, Metrics can be used to access effectiveness of mobile advertising, both financial and non financial metrics are needed to effectively measure performance. Some non financial items , such as market research activities are difficult to measure and companies often avoid measuring those items. However, if the item plays a critical role in delivering organizational value. Measuring it, preferably in quantifiable terms, such as monetary changes or percentages. Even when such measures are difficult to obtain or depend a rough estimates, they provide a basis for examining trends over time and can provide useful information to managers. For example, two metrics for the output awareness are: The number of emails opened recipients and the number of clients that clicked on a promotional mobile advertising. Those two metrics can provide different perspectives on the meaning of awareness, thus the choice of metrics helps clarify the objectives, just as clear objectives can help in identifying specific and to be relevant must be specific and to be relevant they must be customized to meet the unique dynamics of the organization . It aims to achieve the best to capture and reflect the organization's unique sets of activities and results some may be relevant to all organizations and many can be readily adopted to be useful for decision making.

3. Discuss the relationship between mobile advertising and other elements of the promotion in campaign planning in limit advertise time control

Mobile advertisement defines as the use of the mobile medium, it is as a communications and entertainment channel between a brand and an end user. In basic terms, it is the process of planning and execution conception, pricing, promotion and distribution of products and services through the mobile channel. Advertising is a form of communication intended to convince an audience (viewers, readers or listeners) to purchase or take some action upon products, information or services etc. The relationship between independent variables elements and mobile advertising which are environmental response and emotional response with behavioral aspect of consumer buying behavior with mobile advertising. It is time that people purchase those brands with which who are emotionally attached elements. Almost every one grows up in the world which is flooded with the mass media, e.g. television, films, videos, magazines, movies advertising and internet channel is either mobile advertising or computer advertising.

Advertising is a subset of promotion mix which is one of the 4‘p in the marketing mix, i.e. product, price, place and promotion. As a promotional strategy, advertising serve as a major tool in creating product awareness in the mind of a potential consumer to take eventual purchase decision. Advertising, sales promotion and public relations are mass communication tools available to marketers.

Telecommunication technology, such as mobile advertising enables business and industry to grow at a faster pace when contributing to the economic development and at the same time telecommunication infrastructure can be reliable. Cellular phone industry has been one of the profitable businesses in Asian. The country's growing population and huge demand potential have always been an attraction for many high-technological multinational companies. Societies used symbols and pictorial signs to attract their produce users. There elements were used for promotion of products. A company can't make dream to be a well known brand until which invests in their promotional activities for which consumer market have been dominating through advertisements. As the primary mission of advertiser is to reach prospective customers and influence their awareness, attitudes and buying behavior.

The major aim of advertising is to impact on buying behavior, however this impact about brand is changes or strengthened frequently in peoples' memories. Memories about the brand consist of their associations that are related to brand name in consumer mind. These brand cognition influence consideration, evaluation and finally purchases. The promotion in campaign planning to mobile advertising focuses on young people because who choose advertising information and characters as whose role models, who may not only identify with them but also intend to copy them in terms of how who dress and what who are going to buy. As the market is surplus with several products or services, so many companies make similar functional claim, so it has became extremely difficult for companies to differentiate their products or services based on functional attributes alone. Differentiations based on functional attributed, which are shown in advertisement, are never long lasting as the competitors could copy the same. Mobile advertising may differentiate companies‘ products or services promotion channel to attract client's attention, e.g. the company can use movable product images on internet video to show on mobile. However, mobile advertising time ought depend on the business nature, e.g. facial health products target segment is female, so it's mobile advertising time ought choose form 9:00 AM to 6:00 PM working time between Monday to Sunday, due to housewives or working women shall go back home to cook, who shall not turn on mobile phones at home. Hence, if the company had differentiated which brand and it had chose what time is the more popular to accept to let mobile users to turn on their mobile from mobile advertising.

The company mobile advertising will have more promotion effort. For example, if the company sold toys, it's target segment would be 3 ages to 10 ages old. It's mobile advertising ought let every family to find its company website easily. If the family didn't know it's brand, but is was difficult to let the family to find what its toys sale from whose mobile phone because there are many toy companies were using internet advertising to promote which toys. So, it might let every family types " toy" word on yahoo, Google websites, then this toy company name would appear on their websites, the family only clicked its name on their mobile phone, it could show it' toys images, prices, which country manufacturing and which year manufacturing different kind of toys, sale payment and delivery method, e.g. visa card payment, air or land or shipping transportation flight delivery, toys manufacturing ingredients indication from website advertising and it's toys advertising time ought to choose family working time, such as between 9:00 and 6:00 PM , due to who shall bring their mobile to work usually. Hence, the toy company needs to consider family will choose what time to use mobile phone. It ought not choose night time to advertise its toy products from mobile due to family would not turn on whose mobile at home at night time usually. Economic theory has sought to establish relationships between selling prices, sales achieved and consumer's income, similarly before the company chooses to spend mobile advertising expenditure, it ought frequently compared it with sales actual income each month. Social media marketing, such as mobile advertising effectiveness is highly influenced by three aspects: content quality, involvement and integration with the other media platforms methods to assess whether effectiveness of mobile advertising.

On the first aspect, content quality isn't quantity. It shows that managers should not totally reply on the monitoring software to measure and analyze their social media campaign. For example, the twitter website analysis show that some brands/companies, e.g. Microsoft used their Twitter account to connect and to communicate with customers . Their Tweets were about communicating and connecting with their follows, through some personal conversations in subjects. That were relevant to their customers .

As a results, Microsoft clients were able to
beat their main competitors in financial performances and Twitter activities. So, Microsoft can use twitter website to assess whether how many numbers of people use internet service to enter phone, then who decide to buy its software products . If Microsoft found the result of the number of buyers who decide to buy its software from mobile phone Twitter website advertisement channel which is more than mobile phone Yahoo or Google websites advertisement channel after who turn on mobile to see advertising. On the another aspect, building trust and long term relationship to mobile advertising to indicate to how to persuade to increase many shippers to decide to buy any products or seek service, e.g. travel tickets booking service after who use mobile to seek advertising habitually.

Today, media marketing is about building relationship and trust through effective two way communications , e.g. talk about something that customers are interested in and creating products or service that will help to solve customers' problems from mobile advertising. Some of today's social media marketing campaigns are still driven by the old fashioned marketing and focus on short-term effect sales, which is also known as incentive induced behavior. To assess trust and genuine buyer/seller relationships achieved through consistent and engaging conversation will increase the messages (SMM) level of influence. Trust is the key factor to get the followers to actually to something , i.e. change in buying decisions influence their peers and turn it into revenue for the companies. It is crucial to build a strong relationship with customers and enhance brand loyalty. Hence, it implies mobile phone companies need to build trust relationship to let them to pay extract internet charges to aim to read email, news, watch movie habitually. Then, it will increase chance to let potential buyers to prefer to seek advertisement to choose to buy and products or consume service from mobile websites habitually.

Hence, assessment of mobile internet habitual users who use mobile internet time per week from survey is one effective method. Also, firms should start their involvement by inviting their customers or prospects to join their social media community. For example, firms can post the icons of the social media main websites or giving some special deals to customers who become their fans or followers . In the online community, firms should start writing more effective posts. An effective post should reflect honesty and conciseness, it is as key elements of an effective post. It should also be informative to satisfy clients' need for information and experts; opinions. Effective contents should be able to actions from the audience (conversion) so that by the end of this process. Followers will place on order, subscribe newsletter or participate on online surveys. In the offline community, managers should share expertise with their speaker in the local community, which will help to attract more followers or fans and to strength connection with the community. A debate has been going on whether or not consumers are willing to receive mobile advertising. America consumers seem to willing to accept mobile advertising to subsidize the cost of other mobile services , such as email and news services.

A study conducted by HRI Research on behalf of Nokia brand found that the core mobile phone subscriber market (16 to 45 year old) is not only receptive to experiencing mobile advertising, but also actively welcoming mobile advertising in the form of electronic coupons promotion. The relationship between mobile advertising and the four key elements contributing to mobile advertising's acceptance of the promotion in campaign planning. There were mobile advertising should allow users to decide whether or not to receive messages, users could bypass sales messages easily, users should be filter the message received and users want to get mutual benefits of something back. The SMA advertising campaigns of mobile advertising industry plays and consumers have been made afraid of the spam phenomenon deriving from negative email spamming experiences.

The personal nature of the website phone markets spamming especially invasive compared to spam received via other channels and devices. Mobile advertising has the potential to be one of the most powerful one to one digital advertising mediums of utilized in the right manner. SMS trials across the would have show the power of mobile advertising in building direct one to one relationship. The online companies like AT&T, AOC wireless, Microsoft and Nokia to mention few companies that are focused on the potential of mobile marketing via mobile handsets. Factors contributing to the success of mobile advertising include that ability, setting up research. measurement, tracking systems, availability of specialist expertise in agency, service provide and establishing consistent rate mobile cards. Other factors impact of drivers on the development of mobile advertising include that personalized medium, users able to opt in , call to action , i.e. immediate response possible , location specific, interactive profiling, appeals to younger customers , one to many communication.

In conclusion, the relatively between mobile advertising and other elements of the promotion in campaign planning include as below: The first element is by utilizing mobile advertising, companies can run marketing campaigns targeted to tens of thousands of people with a fragment of the costs compared to other direct marketing mediums, such as direct mail or telephone and this in just few seconds of line. The advertising industry uses two types of cost calculation cost per thousand impressions (CPM) and cost per rating point (CPP). CPM is used for both print and electronic media when CPP is more popular for electronic media. For instance, if an advertising campaign costs US$5,000 and has an audience of 300,000 consumers, the CPM will be approximately to the initial CPM measure in media selection , such as quality of the audience, audience attention probability and believability of media selection when the CPM for direct mail is between UA$500 to US$700. For email the CPM ranges from US$5 to US$7.

However when email marketing is losing its efficiency, mobile advertising offers new ways to promote products and services. A significant factor contributing to consumers' willingness to accept mobile advertisement is the capability of mobile handsets to service certain type of messages , such as multimedia messages. Evidently, most consumers in the future will carry on smart phone with them. The smart phones allow advertisers to reach consumers in different locations with personalize messages at a given time. Another element is the industry of SG or 4G network service is faster connection speed is a obvious enables users to receive digital photographs, moving wide images, high quality sound for their mobile handsets. From advertisers; perspective this opens various opportunities to plan and implement more advance m-advertising campaigns and integrate those with existing marketing channels. However, to develop and provide applications, for example, interfaces to the carrier's wireless network need to be provided in multiple areas: location, presence, billing, personalization, provisioning, packet network, transport and messaging systems. Next element is location awareness cab be seen as the driving force of many wireless applications and suits also well types of mobile advertising. When mobile phones are almost always carried with and intelligent location awareness technical solution are available. The final element is personalization means building customer loyalty by building a meaningful one to one relatively by understanding the needs to each individual and helping to satisfy a goal that efficiently and knowledgeably addresses each.

Personalization is about mapping and satisfying of client's goal in specific contest with a business's goal in its respective context. Personalization means understanding different kinds of individual preferences , needs, mindsets and lifestyles and cultural as well as geographical differences. Mobile are already equipment with a profiting options, e.g. silent, meeting, outdoors. For example, the utilization of time and location awareness as personalization variables has the benefit that mobile advertising is a marketing medium has features that other marketing channels lack. Hence, email advertising needs to keep every mobile users' personal information to be confidential, solicited message, relevance to users need and the right frequency.

Reference

Adrian, P. (2012). Introduction to marketing theory & practice, 3 rd edition, London: Oxford press.

Couper, M.P. J. Blair and T. Triplet (1999). A Comparison Of Mail And E-mail For a Survey Of Employees In USA Statistical Agencies. Journal Of Official Statistics, 15, 39-56.

Data monitor (2008). The proctor and gamble company. Retrieved Nov. 15 2009 from http://www.datamonitor.com/

Dyer, D., F. Dalzell & R. Olegario (2004). Rising tide. Lessons learned from 165 years of brand building at Procter and Gamble. Boston, MA: Havard Business School Press.

Priesnitz, W. (2007) Counting Our Food Miles. Natural Life, 1 July.

Sullivan, Nicholas P(2007). You can hear me now: How Micro loans and cell phones are connecting the world, San Francisco, CA: John Wilsey & Sans, 2007.

www.ingramcontent.com/pod-product-compliance
Ingram Content Group UK Ltd.
Pitfield, Milton Keynes, MK11 3LW, UK
UKHW021317160826
14477UKWH00023B/471

9 798885 919982